Teach Me
SPORTS
FOOTBALL

BY BARRY DREAYER

General Publishing Group, Inc.
Los Angeles

Publisher: W. Quay Hays
Editor: Barry Dreayer
Managing Editor: Colby Allerton
Cover Design: Kurt Wahlner
Production Director: Nadeen Torio
Copy Editor: Charles Neighbors

Special thanks to the following individuals for their assistance
with this Football Edition: Vicki Blumenfeld, John Chymczuk,
Paul Joffe, Frank Kleha, John McClain and Jack Reader.

All views and opinions expressed herein are solely those of the
author.

The *Teach Me Sports*™ series is published by General Publishing
Group, Inc., 3100 Airport Avenue, Santa Monica, CA 90405
310-915-9000.

Library Catalog Number 94-078946

ISBN 1-881649-37-7

10 9 8 7 6 5 4 3 2 1

Printed in the USA

INTRODUCTION

To many fanatics, football is more like a religion than a sport. The passion it develops is contagious to those who follow and understand the game. (Would you believe football season tickets are frequently willed from one generation to the next!)

Since there are 22 players on the field at one time, and numerous infractions that may be applicable, football can be overwhelming to the novice fan. That is where *Teach Me Sports Football* comes into play.

This book begins with the assumption that the reader is aware that football involves "players wearing uniforms and helmets who throw, catch, kick and run with the ball." From this basic premise, the book presents a crash course on becoming an educated football fan. It is meant to be used while watching the games on TV and/or in person.

Teach Me Sports Football is based on the professional game played by the National Football League (NFL). Separate sections are devoted to how college football differs.

The book does not attempt to cover every one of football's hundreds of rules and situations, and many examples have been simplified for the sake of clarity. The text shows the WHY behind the WHAT. (For example: Why a screen pass is used when the defense is consistently putting pressure on the quarterback.)

So, come on and join the fun by learning the game!

Teach Me SPORTS
JOIN THE FUN BY LEARNING THE GAME

THE FOOTBALL EDITION

THE ORIGIN OF FOOTBALL

American football is not the brainchild of any one person. It is a modified combination of soccer and rugby that gradually evolved from the two sports.

The first college football game took place on November 6, 1869, in New Brunswick, New Jersey. Rutgers defeated Princeton, 6-4. Each team could play 25 players at a time. Players were not allowed to run carrying the ball, nor could they toss it. They were permitted to butt the ball with their heads, bat it with their hands or kick it.

The first team to score six points won the game. A team scored by kicking the ball across a goal line between two posts stuck in the ground "eight paces" apart.

In 1873 the rules were modified to allow for throwing the ball backward or to the side, similar to modern-day rugby. Walter Camp and Amos Alonzo Stagg were credited with modernizing the game in the 1880s and 1890s. They limited the number of players on the field to 11 for each team, introduced the line of scrimmage, and shaped the field closely to how it looks today.

Eighteen players died and 149 were seriously injured while participating in college football games in 1905. President Theodore Roosevelt threatened to abolish the sport if rough play continued. Therefore two new rules were added:

- The FLYING WEDGE was outlawed. Large players would hold onto suitcase handles sewed to the pants of their teammates, and the ballcarrier would run behind this protective shield. Opponents colliding with a flying wedge risked injury.

- Passing the ball forward was finally allowed, spreading out the action.

The first organized professional league, the American Professional Football Association, formed in 1920. Two years later it changed its name to the National Football League, which still exists today.

Over the next three-quarters of a century, football evolved into the modern-day version enjoyed by millions.

BASIC RULES AND OBJECTIVES OF PROFESSIONAL FOOTBALL

The primary objective is to score more points than the opposing team. There are four different ways to score:

- Touchdown — 6 points
- Point(s) after touchdown conversion (PAT) — 1 or 2 points
- Field goal — 3 points
- Safety — 2 points

(Each of the above methods of scoring will be discussed in detail later)

Each team is allowed 11 players on the field at one time.

- OFFENSE — The team with possession of the football.
- DEFENSE — The team without possession of the football.

A player rarely plays on his team's offense *and* defense. He specializes as either an offensive or defensive player.

If a player is replaced by a substitute, he is allowed to return to the game.

There are 60 minutes of play that are divided into two 30-minute HALVES. HALFTIME is the 12-minute intermission that takes place between each half of play.

- Each half is divided into two 15-minute QUARTERS (or PERIODS).
- Teams switch sides between the first and second quarters and the third and fourth quarters, so no one team will have an advantage for an entire half due to wind direction or the sun.

INCOMPLETE PASS

- Time stops during a game when any of the following occurs:

  - *INCOMPLETE PASS — The ball is thrown forward (FORWARD PASS) to a teammate who fails to catch it within the field of play (nor does an opponent catch it).

  - *A player with possession of the ball steps outside of the playing field (OUT OF BOUNDS).

  - *TEAM TIME OUTS — Each team can stop the clock three times during each half.

  - A foul is called by one of the officials (discussed in detail later).

  - A player is injured on the field and he leaves the game for at least one play.

    1. If an injured player stays in the game for the next play then his team is charged with a time out.

    2. During the last 2 minutes of either half, if a team has already used its 3 team time outs and one of its players is injured, a fourth time out is allowed. If a fifth or more time out is needed in a half because of injury, the team is penalized 5 yards.

       a. If the injury is a result of an illegal act on the part of the opponent such as getting kicked in the stomach, then a fourth or more time out is not charged.

       b. During the last 2 minutes of either half, if the injured player is on the team that has possession of the ball but it has no more team time outs left, an additional time out is allowed—however 10 seconds must be taken off the clock before play can be resumed if the injured player's team is tied or behind in the score. This discourages a team from faking an injury to stop the clock.

11

One would think that the coin toss is the safest part of a football game. Not so on September 22, 1940, if you were to ask Turk Edwards of the Washington Redskins before a game against the New York Giants.

As captain of the Redskins, Edwards went to the center of the field for the coin toss. Edwards won the toss and elected to receive. After he shook hands with the opposing team's captain, he turned to the sidelines and immediately dropped to the ground.

The cleats on the bottom of his shoes got caught in the ground; so when he turned, he severely twisted his knee. The injury was so bad that he never played again.

How do you like that? A football player's career ended, not by an injury involving contact with an opponent, but instead by the coin toss.

- During a PAT conversion.
- To measure whether a first down was achieved (discussed in detail later).
- TWO-MINUTE WARNING — With two minutes remaining in each half, the officials notify each team of the time left.
- TV TIME OUTS — When the network televising the game must show a commercial.
- At the end of each period.
- Whenever teams switch from offense to defense and vice versa.
- Any time the player who receives the ball from the center is tackled behind the line of scrimmage (discussed in detail later).

- It is important to note that the first three ways the clock is stopped (as designated by the *) can be controlled somewhat by the offense, thus playing a role in its strategy late in the game.

COIN TOSS—Three minutes before the game starts, up to 6 designated members of each team (called the CAPTAINS) meet in the middle of the field with the officials for a flip of the coin.

- The winner of the coin toss has the option of choosing:
    - Whether to kick or receive the opening kick-off, or
    - On which side of the field it wants to start in the first quarter.
- Most teams choose to receive when they win the coin toss so that they can try to score first. Therefore, the loser of the coin toss can choose on which side of the field to start.
- At the beginning of the second half, the team that lost the coin toss has first choice of the two options. Once again, the choice generally is to receive the kickoff.

*Allie Sherman, former NY Giants
coach and current broadcaster,
made the following saying famous
after his Giants tied the Dallas
Cowboys in 1965: "A tie is like kiss-
ing your sister."*

● ●

*Bob Zuppke, a former coach at the
University of Illinois, summarized his
thoughts about centers: "No wonder centers
get confused. They're always looking at the
world upside down and backwards."*

If teams are tied after the 60 minutes of regulation play, there is another coin toss to determine who receives the kickoff to begin OVERTIME—an additional period called SUDDEN DEATH.

- After a three-minute intermission, the sudden death period begins and the teams play until one team scores to end the game.
- If neither team scores for 15 minutes, the game ends as a tie (except for playoff games where there must be a winner).
- During the overtime period, each team is entitled to 2 time outs and there is a two-minute warning.

Most parts of the game (called PLAYS) begin by the CENTER handing the football back through his legs (referred to as HIKING, SNAPPING or CENTERING) to the QUARTERBACK who either:

- Runs with the ball.
- Hands the ball to a teammate.
- Throws the ball to a teammate.

Most plays end by (along with an official blowing his whistle):

- A part of the ballcarrier's body (other than his feet or hands) touching the ground as a result of contact with an opposing player.
  - If the ballcarrier trips over his own feet without being touched by an opponent, he can get up and run; the play does not end.
  - If the ballcarrier trips over his own feet and while he is on the ground is touched by an opponent, the play does end.
- An incomplete pass. The next play begins at the same place on the field where the previous play started.
- The ballcarrier stepping out of bounds (which includes stepping on the sidelines that border the length of the field).
- The FORWARD PROGRESS of a ballcarrier being stopped, even if he is not knocked to the ground.

Gene Klein, former owner of the San Diego Chargers, had an interesting point to make about one of his players: "Leon Burns came out of prison....He used to wear a Superman T-shirt under his uniform. After watching him play, I assumed he had gone to jail for false advertising."

The next play begins at the yard line where the opposing team stopped the ballcarrier from moving in a forward direction, ignoring if he was pushed backwards.

- A team scoring.
- A touchback (discussed in detail later) taking place.
- A defensive player gaining possession of the ball after an opponent's muff of a kick or punt (discussed in detail later).
- An offensive player recovering a teammate's fumble (discussed in detail later) in advance of the spot of the fumble either on fourth down or after the two-minute warning in either half.
- A quarterback kneel (discussed in detail later) during the last two minutes of a half.
- A player slides on the ground feet first. This is usually done by a quarterback to avoid contact by an approaching defender.
- A quarterback is in the grasp and control of a defender behind the yard line where the play began.

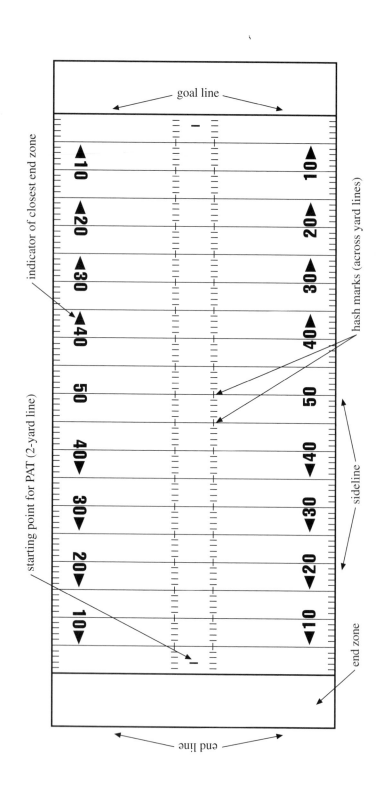

THE PLAYING FIELD

The field (called GRIDIRON by long-time fans) is 120 yards long and 53 ⅓ yards wide.

The 10-yard area at each end of the field is called the END ZONE.

The 100 yards between the two end zones are divided by lines that stretch across the field every five yards. Within each five-yard section are four one-yard indicators.

- Crossing each five-yard line near the center of the field are two short lines (18 1/2 feet apart) called HASH MARKS or INBOUND LINES.
- If a play ends outside of either hash mark, for the next play, the ball is brought to the closest hash mark and then placed on the yard line where the play ended.
- If a play ends between the two hash marks, the next play begins at that place.

Every ten yards are labeled on the field indicating the distance to the closest goal line (10, 20, 30, 40, 50, 40, 30, 20, 10).

- An arrow next to the number on the field points to the closest goal line. While watching a game on television, if the ball is near the 20-yard line, the arrow indicates which 20-yard line.

The SIDELINES border the length of the field from one end zone to the other.

The GOAL POSTS include a base and two vertical bars (UPRIGHTS) connected by a horizontal bar (CROSS-BAR) that is 10 feet above the back line (END LINE) of the end-zone.

- Goal posts used to be located above the GOAL LINES (the front lines of each end zone). They were moved to the back lines of the end zone in 1974 because players would often run into the base

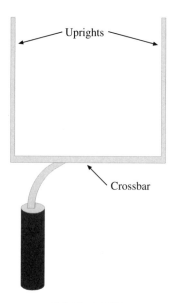

GOAL POST

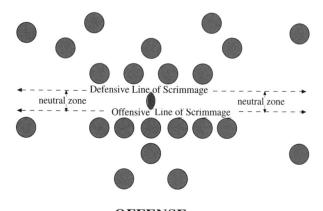

DEFENSE

OFFENSE

LINE OF SCRIMMAGE

of the goal posts while trying to score or prevent a score.

LINE OF SCRIMMAGE — Two imaginary lines drawn across the field intersecting each tip of the football before the play begins.

- The offense and defense each have a line of scrimmage and both must be behind their own line when the ball is hiked.
- The area between each line of scrimmage is the NEUTRAL ZONE.
- Some people refer to the line of scrimmage as the yard line where a play begins.

The 50 yards closest to the goal line that a team is defending is referred to as that team's half of the field. The other 50 yards is the opposing team's half of the field.

- When a football announcer says, "The Jets are on their own 28-yard line," that means they must advance 72 yards (100 - 28) to reach the opponent's goal line.
- When a football announcer says, "The Jets are on the Bears' 28-yard line," that means they only have to advance 28 yards to reach the opponent's goal line.

FIRST DOWN

THE OFFENSE

The short-term objective of the offense is to achieve a FIRST DOWN.

- Upon gaining possession of the football, a team has four plays (or chances) to advance the ball a total of 10 yards.

  - Each play is called a DOWN.

  - If a team succeeds in gaining 10 or more yards in four or less downs, it makes a first down and has four more downs to advance the ball another 10 yards. By making first downs, a team maintains possession of the ball advancing toward the opponent's end zone to score.

    1. Suppose the offense starts its first play on its 20-yard line where it is 1st down and 10 yards to go (for another first down). The offense gains 3 yards to its 23-yard line. It is now 2nd down and 7 yards to go (for another first down).

    2. On the 2nd down play, the offense gains 8 more yards. Mission accomplished! The initial goal of 10 yards has been reached (actually exceeded by one yard). The offense now has 4 more downs to gain another 10 yards. It is once again first down and 10 yards to go.

  - If the team does not succeed in gaining 10 or more yards after 4 downs, the defensive team takes possession of the ball where the fourth down play ended.

  - If the offense has not gained 10 yards after 3 downs, it may consider doing one of the following on fourth down:

    1. PUNT the ball to the opposing team to force the opponent's possession of the ball to begin further down the field. Punting is when a player kicks the ball after he releases it from his hands but before it touches the ground.

TOUCHDOWN

• •

*Kickers are famous for their
excuses after an unsuccessful field
goal attempt. How about former Dallas
Cowboys kicker, Rafael Septien, after
one of his attempts went wide of the goal
posts: Septien turned to his holder, Danny
White, and complained, "No wonder.
You placed the ball upside down."*

2. Attempt a FIELD GOAL if the ball is close enough to the opponent's end zone (usually within 40 yards). When a team's field goal kicker kicks the ball from the ground through the uprights of the goal posts, it is a successful field goal.

   a. The kicking team scores three points on a successful field goal.

   b. If the kick does not go through the uprights, the opposing team gains possession of the ball at the yard line where the kick was attempted or the 20-yard line, whichever is furthest from the end zone. However, if the opposing team touches the ball beyond the line of scrimmage, or if the field goal attempt is blocked (deflected) and the ball ends up behind the line of scrimmage, the next play begins where the kicking play ends.

The offense's long-term objective is to score a TOUCHDOWN. When a player has possession of the ball in the opposing team's end zone, a touchdown is scored. The most common ways for an offensive player to score a touchdown are:

- A player runs into the end zone while holding the ball.
- A player catches a pass in the end zone while both feet are touching the ground or while jumping and then landing with both feet touching the ground in the end zone.
- A player RECOVERS A FUMBLE in the defending team's end zone. A fumble recovery occurs when a player gains possession of the football after another player who had possession drops the ball. Here are two exceptions:
  - On fourth down, a fumble by an offensive player that is recovered by his teammate in the defending team's end zone is brought

Offensive linemen very rarely receive praise for their work by the fans and media. Former Raiders guard, Gene Upshaw, expressed his frustration: "I've compared offensive linemen to the story of Paul Revere. After Paul Revere rode through town, everybody said what a great job he did. But no one ever talked about the horse."

● ●

DEFENSE

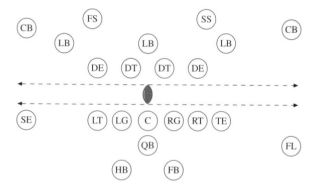

OFFENSE
STANDARD OFFENSE/DEFENSE

SE= SPLIT END	TE= TIGHT END	DT= DEFENSIVE
LT= LEFT TACKLE	FL= FLANKER	TACKLE
LG= LEFT GUARD	HB= HALFBACK	LB= LINEBACKER
C= CENTER	FB= FULLBACK	CB= CORNERBACK
RG= RIGHT GUARD	QB= QUARTERBACK	SS= STRONG SAFETY
RT= RIGHT TACKLE	DE=DEFENSIVE END	FS= FREE SAFETY

back to where the fumble took place. No touchdown is scored.

- On any down after the two-minute warning, a fumble by an offensive player that is recovered by his teammate in the defending team's end zone is brought back to where the fumble took place. No touchdown is scored.

Here's how a team gains possession of the football for its offense:

- Preventing the opposing team's offense from advancing the ball ten yards or from scoring after four downs.
- Catching an opponent's forward pass, called an INTERCEPTION.
- Recovering an opponent's fumble. Note that the ground cannot cause a fumble. If the ball-carrier is TACKLED (discussed in detail later) and as he hits the ground, the impact causes him to lose possession of the football, it is not a fumble. The play ends at the point of impact with the ground.
- Receiving a punt from the opposing team.
- Receiving a KICKOFF from the opposing team.
    1. An opposing player "kicks off" the ball that is placed on a plastic kicking TEE on his own 30-yard line. A kickoff occurs after a team scores or at the beginning of each half (and overtime).
- An opposing team missing a field goal attempt.

The players on offense:

- Five INTERIOR LINEMEN — The primary role of an interior lineman is to BLOCK his defensive opponents by using his body to protect a teammate who has the ball.

- Interior linemen must begin each play on the line of scrimmage.
- Interior linemen generally weigh between 275 and 325 pounds.
- Interior linemen include:

DEFENSE

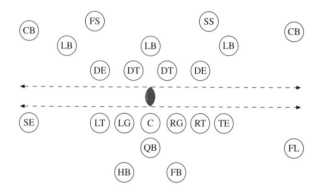

OFFENSE
STANDARD OFFENSE/DEFENSE

• •

*Hunter Thompson, the political writer,
gave his thoughts about tight ends:
"The only other group I've dealt with who
struck me as being essentially meaner
than politicians are tight ends
in pro football."*

1. One CENTER — Initiates each play by hiking the ball through his legs to the quarterback, punter or holder for a field goal or PAT attempt.

2. Two GUARDS — Two players who surround the center. They are usually the quickest of the interior linemen. Some plays are designed for both guards to run ahead of the ballcarrier and block for him.

3. Two TACKLES — Two players who line up outside of the guards and are usually the biggest of the linemen. A play that is designed for the ballcarrier to run behind one of the tackles is called an OFF TACKLE play.

- Two ENDS
  - TIGHT END — Lines up at one end of the line of scrimmage next to one of the tackles. That side of the offensive line is called the STRONG SIDE.

    1. Catches passes and blocks. Therefore, he must be relatively big, but also athletic and coordinated to catch the football.

    2. Because he often catches passes in the center of the field near many defensive players, the tight end must be prepared for some "bumps and bruises."

  - SPLIT END — Lines up at the end of the line of scrimmage on the opposite side from the tight end. That side of the offensive line is called the WEAK SIDE.

    1. Usually lines up a few yards away from the closest tackle leaving him more room to catch passes, which is his primary responsibility.

    2. Frequently one of the fastest players on the team. His speed helps him get away from a defender to catch a pass.

    3. Blocks during plays when another

DEFENSE

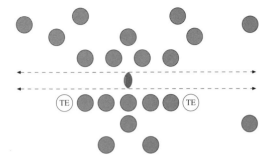

OFFENSE

2 TIGHT ENDS

(NO SPLIT ENDS)

• •

DEFENSE

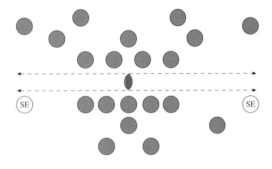

OFFENSE

2 SPLIT ENDS

(NO TIGHT ENDS)

• •

*James Lofton, a wide receiver with
a long career in professional football,
talked about his position: "Two guys were
talking about a guy who catches well
in a crowd. To me it just means
he can't get open."*

teammate is carrying the ball.

- There must be a minimum of 7 offensive players lined up so that some part of their helmet is between the center's waist and their line of scrimmage: 5 interior linemen (including the center) and the 2 ends.

- A team can use 2 tight ends or 2 split ends instead of one of each.

    1. When might a team use two tight ends in the game?

        a. If three or less yards are needed for a first down or touchdown and the offense wants the bulk of an extra tight end to assist in blocking for the ballcarrier.

    2. When might a team have two split ends in the game?

        a. If four or more yards are needed for a first down or touchdown and the offense wants the speed of an extra split end to slip away from a defender.

- BACKS — Players who line up in the BACKFIELD (behind an imaginary line from sideline to sideline running through the center's waist) and the player who receives the snap from the center.

    - No more than 4 players can be in the backfield because 7 of the offense's 11 players must be on the line of scrimmage.

    - One back is allowed to move backward or parallel to the line of scrimmage while the ball is being snapped. He is sometimes referred to as the MAN IN MOTION.

    - The backs include:

        1. Two RUNNING BACKS who are eligible to catch passes.

            a. HALFBACK — He runs with the ball more often than he blocks during running plays, so he is usually the faster running back.

            b. FULLBACK — Blocks more often

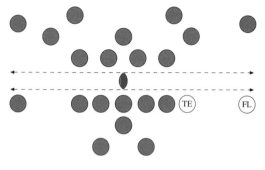

TIGHT END INELIGIBLE

If the flanker lined up on the line of scrimmage outside of the tight end, the tight end would be an ineligible receiver for not being on the end of the line of scrimmage.

• •

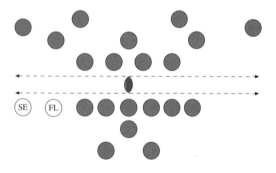

FLANKER INELIGIBLE

If the flanker lined up on the line of scrimmage between the split end and tackle, the flanker himself would be an ineligible receiver for not being on the end of the line of scrimmage.

than he runs with the ball during running plays, so he is usually the bigger running back.

2. One FLANKER — Very similar to the split end (eligible to catch passes and usually lines up a few yards away from the closest tackle), but he lines up in the backfield. Why? Because the only players on the line of scrimmage who are allowed to catch passes are the outermost players on the right and left side—the ends. If he lined up on the line of scrimmage, either he would be an ineligible receiver or he would make another player ineligible to catch passes.

   a. The flanker and split end are referred to as WIDE RECEIVERS.

   b. Sometimes a team may use 2 flankers and remove one of the running backs if it wants to emphasize passing.

– One QUARTERBACK — Player in charge of the offense on the field. Must have a strong and accurate throwing arm because he throws most of the passes.

1. Before each play, most teams gather in a circular HUDDLE, where the quarterback gives instructions as to how each player should line up and what they should do after the ball is snapped. These instructions are given in a short code and are either the quarterback's decision or that of his coach. Plays from the coach are usually relayed to the quarterback by an in-helmet electronic system.

   a. The coach's headset has a transmitter.

   b. The quarterback's helmet has two receivers, one for each ear.

   c. The communication is only one way—from coach to quarterback.

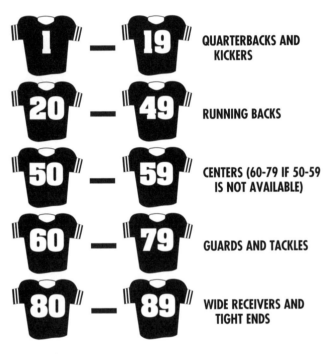

1 — 19 QUARTERBACKS AND KICKERS

20 — 49 RUNNING BACKS

50 — 59 CENTERS (60-79 IF 50-59 IS NOT AVAILABLE)

60 — 79 GUARDS AND TACKLES

80 — 89 WIDE RECEIVERS AND TIGHT ENDS

OFFENSIVE PLAYERS

d. The system automatically shuts off with 15 seconds remaining on the PLAY clock (discussed in detail later).

2. The players leave the huddle and the quarterback READS THE DEFENSE, checking out where the defensive players are positioned (called ALIGNMENT).

3. If the quarterback thinks that the play will not work because of the defensive alignment, he may change the play through a set of prearranged verbal signals called an AUDIBLE.

4. The quarterback takes the ball from the center and either gives the ball to a teammate (usually a running back), passes the ball to a teammate (a back or an end) or runs with the ball himself.

JERSEY NUMBERS – Players on offense must wear numbers according to their position as illustrated on the opposite page. If an offensive player is to play a position that has different pass-receiving eligibility from what his jersey number indicates, he must first report to the referee before going in the huddle. The referee then notifies the defense. (A guard wearing number 66 switching to running back must first notify the referee.)

Joe Kapp, a former quarterback with the Minnesota Vikings, after getting sacked numerous times during a game, reflected back, "I remember it was a beautiful day because I spent most of it lying on my back looking up at the blue sky."

● ●

DEFENSE

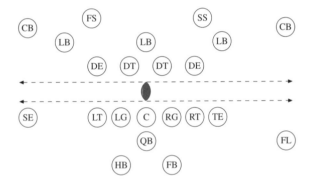

OFFENSE

STANDARD OFFENSE/DEFENSE

SE= SPLIT END	TE= TIGHT END	DT= DEFENSIVE
LT= LEFT TACKLE	FL= FLANKER	TACKLE
LG= LEFT GUARD	HB= HALFBACK	LB= LINEBACKER
C= CENTER	FB= FULLBACK	CB= CORNERBACK
RG= RIGHT GUARD	QB= QUARTERBACK	SS= STRONG SAFETY
RT= RIGHT TACKLE	DE=DEFENSIVE END	FS= FREE SAFETY

THE DEFENSE

The defense's short-term objective is to prevent the offense of the opposing team from achieving a first down.

The defense's long-term objective is to prevent the offense of the opposing team from scoring.

The defense is always at a disadvantage because it doesn't know which play the opposing team's offense will run. The ability to react is essential to a successful defense.

The players on defense:

- DEFENSIVE LINEMEN — Usually 3 or 4 large (275 pounds or more) players who line up on their line of scrimmage.

  - Responsible for TACKLING the ballcarrier, which means pulling or knocking him down so that any part of his body (other than just his hands or feet) touches the ground. When a quarterback is tackled while attempting to pass the ball, it is called a SACK.

  - If not able to sack the quarterback, they still want to get near him so that he will hurry his throw, causing an incomplete pass (sometimes called an INCOMPLETION) or interception.

  - Must first avoid or move players on offense who may be blocking their path to the ballcarrier.

  - Unlike offensive linemen, defensive linemen can use their hands to move opposing players out of their way.

  - Some teams use four defensive linemen — two DEFENSIVE TACKLES and two DEFENSIVE ENDS. The defensive ends line up outside of the defensive tackles and are usually quicker. Other teams use three defensive linemen—two defensive ends and a NOSE GUARD who sets up in the middle of the defensive line opposite the offensive center.

DEFENSE

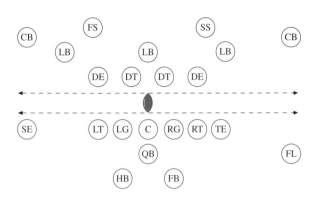

OFFENSE
STANDARD OFFENSE/DEFENSE

• •

Linebackers are tough football players. Here are a couple of comments about these fierce warriors:

Former Green Bay Packers linebacker Ray Nitschke described himself as follows: "Each time I tackled somebody, I tried to make sure that when he got up and walked away he'd remember he'd met Ray Nitschke. And I don't mean socially."

• •

Ahmad Rashad, currently a sports broadcaster and one-time wide receiver with the Buffalo Bills and Minnesota Vikings, had this to say about linebackers: "Linebackers are the strangest guys of all....They're people who just plain love to run into things. They'll hit you as you go by them the way other people shake hands."

– Certain situations dictate using more than four defensive linemen. When?

1. If the offense has only three or less yards to go for a first down or touchdown, the defense, anticipating a running play, will place more players on the line of scrimmage.

– The area where offensive and defensive linemen "butt heads" is sometimes referred to as the TRENCHES or the PITS.

- LINEBACKERS — Three or four players who position themselves in back of the defensive linemen. Usually are faster and 30-50 pounds lighter than the defensive linemen.

– Help defend against a pass, usually to a running back.

– Attempt to tackle the ballcarrier.

– At times a linebacker joins the defensive linemen rushing in to sack the quarterback. This is called a BLITZ or RED DOG.

– When there are three linebackers, the MIDDLE LINEBACKER is between the two OUTSIDE LINEBACKERS. With four linebackers, the two in the middle are called INSIDE LINEBACKERS.

- DEFENSIVE BACKS — Generally four players (but often five or six are used in obvious passing situations) who position themselves near one of the offensive receivers. Usually 20 to 30 pounds lighter than linebackers and much faster.

– Two CORNERBACKS

1. Prevent their assigned wide receiver from catching the ball, or if possible, they intercept it.

2. Help tackle the ballcarrier if a defensive linemen or linebacker is unable to do so.

a. It is a bad sign if cornerbacks are making a lot of tackles.

b. Cornerbacks are frequently led away

JERSEY NUMBERS — Generally defensive players wear numbers according to their position as illustrated above.

DEFENSIVE BACKS

LINEBACKERS
(90-99 IF 50-59 IS NOT AVAILABLE)

DEFENSIVE LINEMEN
(90-99 IF 60-79 IS NOT AVAILABLE)

DEFENSIVE PLAYERS

• •

Dick Butkus set the standard for meanness when he played for the Chicago Bears from 1965-1973. In a game against the Detroit Lions, as he wrapped his arms around Lions tight end Charlie Sanders, Butkus stuck his fingers through Sanders face mask to poke his eyes out.

Butkus on-field play can be summarized with his own comment: "I wouldn't ever want to hurt anybody deliberately, unless it was important—like a league game or something."

from the line of scrimmage by one of the receivers. If they end up tackling the ballcarrier, it will probably be after a number of yards have been gained.

- Two SAFETIES

    1. STRONG SAFETY — Normally responsible for the tight end. (Remember that the side of the line of scrimmage where the tight end lines up is the strong side.)

    2. FREE or WEAK SAFETY — Free to roam and follow the ball.

        a. Usually not responsible for any specific offensive player.

        b. At times may blitz the quarterback.

    3. Both safeties tackle the ballcarrier, if necessary.

Steve O'Neal of the 1969 New York Jets had a memorable punt on September 21, 1969 against the Denver Broncos. The Jets were on their own 1-yard line on fourth down, when O'Neal entered the game. He punted the ball over 70 yards in the air bouncing at the Broncos' 30-yard line. The ball continued to bounce until it stopped on the Broncos' 1-yard line—a punt of 98 yards. That is where the Broncos' offense took over.

O'Neal's punt was the most effective one in history. With his team backed up to its 1-yard line, one "swing of the leg" by O'Neal backed up the opponents to their 1-yard line.

THE SPECIAL TEAMS

The players on the field during a play when the ball is kicked or punted.

Most special team players are the team's RESERVES (those who don't start the game on offense or defense).

Very important players—approximately ⅓ of the points in a game are scored while they are on the field.

The following plays involve special teams:

- Kickoffs — Football usually kicked off a plastic TEE (which elevates the ball one inch off the ground) at the kicking team's 30-yard line. Remember that kickoffs take place after a team scores and at the beginning of each half (and overtime).

    - Receiving team must stand at least 10 yards away until the ball is kicked. Once the ball travels 10 yards, it is a FREE BALL and either team can try to gain possession. If a kickoff touches a player on the receiving team, even before it has traveled 10 yards, it is also a free ball.

    - Receiving team frequently positions one or two players (KICKOFF RETURNERS) at its goal line, anticipating a long kick in order to catch the ball and run it back.

    - Kicking team must stand behind its 30-yard line until the ball is kicked.

- Punts — The center hikes the ball to the PUNTER standing about 12 to 15 yards behind him, giving the punter time to kick the ball before a defender can get to him. A good blocker on the punting team sets up in the backfield to block any onrushing defensive players who "bust through" the offensive line.

    - If an offensive team fails in three downs to advance the ball ten yards, it may choose to punt the ball. The purpose of the punt is

Roland Hooks, a special team player for the Buffalo Bills in the 1980's, was not a big fan of that duty: "Returning punts is not a job I can get excited about. Most of the things that can happen to you are negative. One, you can fumble. Two, you can get slammed down in your tracks. Three, you can come up fast on a punt and run into your own man. Four, you can be second-guessed for not signaling for a fair catch. And five, you can get a concussion. You risk all this for maybe eight yards."

to give the receiving team possession of the ball further away from the punting team's goal line.

- The offense might choose not to punt after three downs when the team:

   1. Is close enough to the other team's goal posts to attempt a field goal for three points.

   2. Only needs a yard or two for a first down. However, if the offense has possession of the ball on its side of the fifty-yard line, it is not worth the risk of failing and giving the opposing team such great FIELD POSITION.

   3. Is losing late in the fourth quarter and the team needs to score. A fourth down attempt gives the team a chance to score. If the fourth down attempt fails, the opponent gains possession of the ball (the same result as a punt on fourth down which does not give the offensive team a chance to score). When time is a factor, scoring is the priority of the team that is losing.

- A punter's average punt ends up between 40 to 50 yards from the line of scrimmage. The punt's HANG TIME, the time the ball stays in the air, is important. The more hang time, the better chance the punting team can be downfield to defend against the receiving team returning the punt.

- A PUNT RETURNER positions himself downfield awaiting the punt. He can:

   1. Catch the ball and run with it.

   2. Signal for a FAIR CATCH by waving his hand back and forth while the punt is in the air. (A kickoff returner can also signal for a fair catch, but seldom does.) A fair catch means that:

      a. The punt returner cannot run with the ball once he catches it. (If the ball touches the ground, even if the

Ron Widby, the punter on the 1969 Dallas Cowboys, was uniquely involved from start to finish on a punt play during a game against the St. Louis Cardinals.

Widby's punt went off the side of his foot, causing it to travel only a few yards, taking some weird bounces. Widby ran up to the line of scrimmage where the bouncing ball found Widby right between his hands. He caught his own punt, giving the Cardinals a first and ten at the yard line where Widby touched (downed) the football.

• •

The Buffalo Bills kicker in 1966, Booth Lusteg, failed on a relatively easy 23-yard field goal attempt. The score was tied with less than a minute left in the game, so the three points would have likely won the game for the Bills. Instead the game ended in a tie.

After the game, Lusteg was walking from the stadium when a car stopped next to him and four mad Bills fans jumped out. After confirming that he was Booth Lusteg, one of the fans slugged him in the mouth.

When police questioned Lusteg about the incident, he refused to talk. Later asked why he did not tell police about the incident, he responded, "I had it coming."

punt returner drops it, anyone on the punt returning team can advance with the ball.)

 b. The punting team cannot touch the punt returner or interfere with him catching the ball. The punt returner signals for a fair catch on a punt that has a lengthy hang time (4 or more seconds) to protect himself from being hit immediately after he catches the ball.

 c. The receiving team begins its offensive series at the yard line where the punt returner catches the ball. Instead of a fair catch, if the punt returner allows the ball to hit the ground, the ball could bounce toward his goal line giving his team poorer field position.

– If no one on the receiving team touches the punted ball (and the ball does not go beyond the receiving team's goal line—discussed in detail later), the offensive series begins where the ball:

 1. Is touched (DOWNED) by a member of the punting team.

 2. Goes out of bounds.

 3. Stops on the playing field.

– Only the 2 players on the punting team closest to each sideline can run downfield once the ball is snapped. All other members of the punting team must wait until the ball is punted.

• Field goal attempt.

– A team may try to kick the ball through the goal posts on the fourth down if the offense is close to the other team's end zone.

– Most teams have a field goal kicker (called PLACEKICKER) who can accurately kick the ball off the ground 50 yards away from the goal posts. (Some placekickers can kick even longer field goals).

placekicker

holder

KICKER/HOLDER

•••••••••••••••••••••••••••••••

*When looking up the word
"automatic" in the dictionary, do not
be surprised to see a picture of former
San Francisco 49er placekicker, Tommy
Davis, next to the definition. From
1959-1965, Davis successfully kicked
234 consecutive PATs without a
miss—an NFL record.*

*During Davis's career, the
goal posts were positioned on the goal
line. A PAT for Davis was like kicking a
9-yard field goal (the 2-yard line where
the ball is placed for PATs plus the 7 yards
behind the line of scrimmage where the
holder usually places the ball). Currently,
the goal posts are 10 yards behind the
goal line, so a PAT is like kicking a
19-yard field goal.*

– During a field goal attempt, the kicking team does the following:

1. The center hikes the ball to the HOLDER (usually the team's punter or reserve quarterback) who kneels about 7 yards behind the line of scrimmage to minimize the chance of the kick being blocked.

   a. If the line of scrimmage is the opposing team's 30-yard line, on fourth down the offensive team may try a 47-yard field goal (add 10 yards because the goal posts are 10 yards back in the end zone plus another 7 yards to account for where the holder usually kneels).

2. The holder catches the ball and quickly places it on the ground with the laces of the football away from the kicker.

3. Most kickers approach the ball and kick it with the inside of their foot, called SOCCER STYLE. Very few kickers use the conventional style of kicking the ball with the top of their foot, which is a less powerful kick.

– The rules indicate that a field goal may be attempted by using a DROPKICK; the kicker "drops" the ball and kicks it as it hits the ground. A dropkick is never used in football today.

• PAT conversion attempt.

– Occurs after a touchdown and begins on the 2-yard line.

– A team has the option to:

1. Kick the ball, similar to a field goal, for one point.

2. Try to cross the goal line from the 2-yard line on a running or passing play scoring two points.

SAFETY

• •

One of the most unusual safeties in football history took place on October 25, 1964, in a game between the Minnesota Vikings and the San Francisco 49ers. Here's what happened: San Francisco quarterback George Mira completed a pass to his running back, Billy Kilmer, who fumbled the ball after being hit by a defender. Minnesota Viking defensive end, Jim Marshall, who had been running toward the quarterback, turned around and picked up the loose ball. Unfortunately, he started running to his own goal line.

After he reached his goal line, his teammate, Fran Tarkenton, yelled from the sidelines and pointed toward the 49er goal line. Marshall's confused response was to throw the ball out of bounds toward the waving Tarkenton, causing a safety. Marshall's blunder did not cause the Vikings to lose that afternoon, as they beat the 49ers 27-22. But Marshall will never forget the embarrassing safety.

TERMS AND DEFINITIONS

SAFETY — Two points are awarded to the defensive team (who then receives a punt, kickoff or dropkick from the opposing team's 20-yard line) when any one of the following happens:

- An offensive ballcarrier is tackled in his own end zone.
- An offensive ballcarrier steps out of or fumbles the ball out of either side, or the back of his end zone.
- The punting team has a punt blocked and the ball goes out of either side or the back of its end zone, including touching the goal posts or crossbar.
- Certain penalties are committed by the offensive team in its end zone.

> **General Rule:** If a player on a team "caused" the ball to be in his end zone (or go out of either side, or the back of his end zone) when the play ended, it is a safety.

TOUCHBACK — A play that ends in a team's own end zone, entitling that team to begin its offensive series with a first down on its own 20-yard line. No points are awarded. Occurs when one of the following happens:

- A kickoff or punt crosses the goal line and is not run out of the end zone by the receiving team.
- A pass is intercepted by a defender who does not run it out of his end zone.
    - If a defender intercepts a pass in his end zone, tries to run it out, but is tackled in his end zone, it is a touchback.
    - However, if a defender intercepts a pass in his end zone, tries to run it out, but fumbles and the opposing team recovers the ball in the end zone, it is a touchdown for the opposing team.
- A defender recovers a fumble in his own end zone. (If an offensive player recovers a fumble in his own end zone, it is a safety.)

DEFENSE

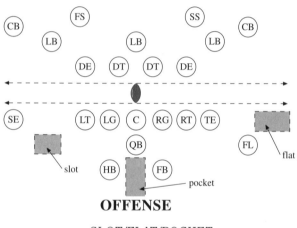

OFFENSE

SLOT/FLAT/POCKET

●●●●●●●●●●●●●●●●●●●●●●●●●●●●●●●●●●●

When John McKay was the Tampa Bay Buccaneers coach, he was asked about his team's execution after losing 26 straight games. His reply: "I'm in favor of it."

- A kickoff or punt touches the receiving team's goal posts or crossbar.

> **General Rule:** If a player on a team did not "cause" the ball to be in his end zone (or go out of either side, or the back of his end zone) when the play ended, it is a touchback.

FLAT — The areas of the playing field near the sidelines, close to the line of scrimmage.

POCKET — 7 to 10 yards behind the center, where the quarterback likes to drop back and throw. The offensive linemen and running backs surround the pocket to protect the quarterback as he throws.

SLOT — The area between a wide receiver and a tackle, but a yard or two behind the line of scrimmage. This is where some running backs or flankers line up when they are going to try to catch a pass.

TURNOVER — An interception, a fumble or a muff that is lost to the opposing team.

EXECUTION — The performance of a team's strategy.

MEASUREMENT — The officials bring out the "sticks and chain" to determine if a first down has been achieved.
- One stick (or pole) is placed at the line of scrimmage where it was first down.
- The other stick (connected by a 10-yard chain) is then stretched out near the ball.
- If any part of the ball is even with or extends past that stick, it is a first down.

CHAIN GANG — The officials who are in charge of carrying the first down measuring sticks.

HANDOFF — A player (usually the quarterback) hands the ball to a teammate (most likely a running back) to run with it.

*On September 24, 1950,
quarterback Jim Hardy of the
Chicago Cardinals had a "night-
mare" day. He had a car accident
on the way to the stadium. Hardy
then arrived at the stadium just
before kickoff so he did not have
time to throw any passes before-
hand to warm up. It showed.*

*Hardy threw a record 8
interceptions during the game
in which his team lost to the
Philadelphia Eagles 45-7. In the
middle of the third quarter, his
coach, Curley Lambeau, replaced
him with the team's other quarterback who suffered a knee
injury 3 plays later. Hardy had to
come back into the game to finish
his humiliating experience.*

*During the game, Hardy
threw the ball 39 times, completing 12 to his teammates and
you know the rest.*

LATERAL or BACKWARD PASS — A ball tossed backward or to the side by a player (usually the quarterback) to a teammate (most likely a running back). A lateral can be thrown underhand or overhand, and can take place anywhere on the playing field (including beyond the line of scrimmage).

FORWARD PASS — A ball tossed forward by a player (usually the quarterback) to one of his backs or ends.

- Only one forward pass is allowed during each play and the thrower must be behind the line of scrimmage.
- Once the ball crosses the line of scrimmage, a forward pass cannot be thrown, even if the ball is brought back behind the line of scrimmage during the play.

RECEPTION—A forward pass that is caught by an offensive player.

- Sometimes called a COMPLETION.
- Both feet or any other part of the receiver's body (not counting his hands) must touch the ground inbounds before and after the catch to count as a reception. Otherwise it is an incomplete pass.
- If a receiver jumps to catch the ball and is pushed out of bounds by a defender, but an official believes that the receiver would have landed in bounds had he not been pushed, it is a reception.

INTERCEPTION—A forward pass that is caught by a defensive player.

- Both feet or any other part of the defender's body (not counting his hands) must touch the ground inbounds before and after the catch to count as an interception. Otherwise it is an incomplete pass.
- If a defender jumps to catch the ball and is pushed out of bounds by an opponent, but an official believes that the defender would have landed in bounds had he not been pushed, it is an interception.

On September 10, 1978, the Oakland Raiders had a fumble that forced a change in the rule books. Here's how:

The Raiders were losing to the San Diego Chargers 20-14 with only 10 seconds left in the game. From the Charger's 14-yard line, Raider quarterback Kenny Stabler took the snap and while looking for a receiver, got hit from behind. On his way to the ground, he flicked his wrist causing the fumbled ball to go forward.

At the 8-yard line, teammate Pete Banaszak batted and kicked the ball to the end zone, while giving the impression he was trying to pick the ball up. Another teammate Dave Casper "accidentally" kicked the ball a bit further so that he could recover the ball in the end zone, which he did for the game-winning touchdown (the PAT was successful).

The next year the league added the rule that after the 2-minute warning, a fumble may not be advanced by the fumbling team, unless the player who fumbled recovered the ball.

• •

Former Kansas City Chief quarterback (and current broadcaster) Len Dawson set the NFL record for most fumbles lost in a game on November 15, 1964, against the San Diego Chargers. During the game, Dawson fumbled the ball 7 times and the Chargers recovered.

Is it not surprising to find out that the conditions of the game resembled a flood? Dawson's comments after the game were: "It was raining so hard the water was going up my nose. One time, I almost drowned when I got hit and they buried my face in a puddle of water."

FUMBLE — A dropped ball by a player who had possession of the football. A fumble can be advanced by any player who picks it up.

- If a player intentionally fumbles the ball forward, it is ruled an incomplete pass.
- An intentional fumble is not always easy to determine, therefore the following rules were added:
  - If a player fumbles on fourth down and a teammate recovers, the next play begins:
    1. On the yard line where the fumble occurred, if the ball was recovered ahead of that yard line. The offense is not able to gain an advantage by a fourth down fumble.
    2. On the yard line where the recovery took place if it is behind where the ball was fumbled.
  - If a player fumbles after the two-minute warning and a teammate recovers, the next play begins:
    1. On the yard line where the fumble occurred, if the ball was recovered ahead of that yard line. The offense is not able to gain an advantage by a fumble after the two-minute warning.
    2. On the yard line where the recovery took place if it is behind where the ball was fumbled.

MUFF — A ball touched by a player in an unsuccessful attempt to gain possession of it, such as dropping a punt. A muff (other than of a backward pass) cannot be advanced by an opposing player who recovers it.

- Many times a punt returner drops a punt and a player on the opposing team picks it up and runs to the end zone thinking he had scored. Not so, because the play ends at the place where the muffed punt is recovered by an opposing player.

BREAK A TACKLE — A ballcarrier avoids an opposing player who touched him while attempting a tackle.

Positive thinking is an important trait of a successful football player. Former college coach, Charlie Pell, stressed this point: "I want my players to think as positively as the eighty-five-year-old man who married a twenty-five-year-old woman and ordered a five-bedroom house near an elementary school."

BREAK THE PLANE — The ball held by a player touches an imaginary vertical plane, the base of the plane being the opponent's goal line. The result is a touchdown, no matter what happens after the ballcarrier breaks the plane (including getting pushed back to the 1-yard line).

FIRST AND GOAL (TO GO) — A first down is achieved within 10 yards of the opponent's goal line. The offensive team's next target is the goal line for a touchdown. That is why it is called "goal to go."

COACHES — Direct the actions of the players on the field — the "bosses" of the team.

- HEAD COACH — Primarily responsible for the team. He has assistant coaches to help him.
- During the game some coaches stand on the sidelines near the field, while others sit upstairs in the press box where they have a better view of the game. The "upstairs" coaches communicate with the "field" coaches through headphones.

On December 8, 1968, the Los Angeles Rams had a first down and ten yards to go against the Chicago Bears, with less than a minute remaining in the game. The Rams were guilty of an offensive holding foul on the next play, and the penalty was accepted by the Bears. Rams quarterback, Roman Gabriel, then threw three straight incomplete passes.

The officials gave the ball to the Bears thinking the Rams had used its four downs without gaining ten yards. The Bears ran a play that used up the final 10 seconds to win the game.

The officials, fans, players or coaches did not realize until after the game that Los Angeles should have been given another down. (Remember that the down remains the same when a penalty for offensive holding is accepted.) It was too late to correct the situation, and the Bears' victory counted.

FOULS AND PENALTIES

A PENALTY is the punishment given to a team for violating the rules, committing a FOUL. A penalized team is usually punished by an official moving the ball back toward its goal line.

(Note: The term "foul" is rarely used by broadcasters to describe a rule violation. Instead, they use the term "penalty," to describe both the violation and the punishment. To make it easier to understand, *Teach Me Sports Football* will refer to the actual violation as a "foul" and the punishment as a "penalty.")

Officials who see a foul being committed by a team immediately drop a gold handkerchief (called a FLAG). When the play is over, the referee explains the options of accepting or DECLINING (refusing to accept) the penalty to the other team.

- The team that was fouled can decline a penalty if it is better off with the results of the play.

In most cases, if a penalty is accepted by a team, the number of the down remains the same as it was before the penalty.

- Suppose it is second down, 8 yards to go for a first down and the offensive team is guilty of a 5-yard penalty from the line of scrimmage. If the penalty is accepted, the next play is still second down but 13 yards to go.

- *What should be done in the following situation?* It is first down 10 yards to go. The offense gains 7 yards on the next play during which the defense is guilty of a 5-yard penalty that is marked off from the original line of scrimmage. The choice to accept or decline a penalty is not always obvious. The team can:

    - Decline the penalty resulting in second down and 3 yards to go, or

    - Accept the 5-yard penalty resulting in first down and 5 yards to go. (The down remains the same as it was before the penalty.)

PERSONAL FOUL

Some penalties against the defensive team give the offensive team an automatic first down, no matter how many yards were needed to gain a first down.

If a penalty would move the ball more than half the distance to either goal line, then the penalty is stepped off to that halfway point and no further.

- For example, if a team is at its own 6-yard line and it is called for a 5-yard penalty, the team would only be penalized back to its 3-yard line—half the distance to the goal line.

- Suppose a team is at the opponent's 24-yard line and the opponents were guilty of a 15-yard penalty, the next play would begin at the 12-yard line—half the distance to the goal line.

If both teams commit a foul during a play in which possession of the ball did not change, the result is usually OFFSETTING PENALTIES and the down is replayed.

- However, if one team's penalty is 15 yards and the other team's penalty is 5 yards only (not an automatic first down or loss of down), the 15-yard penalty is enforced. The penalties do not offset.

If the defense commits a foul during a play when time for a quarter expires, by accepting the penalty the offense can extend the quarter another play to replay the down.

- If the foul by the defense occurs at the end of the first or third quarter, the offense can choose to have the penalty enforced at the beginning of the next quarter. (Wind direction for an attempted field goal might be a factor in this decision.)

- If the offense commits a foul during a play when time for a quarter expires, the quarter ends.

Fouls that are frequently committed include:

- CLIPPING — A player blocks an opposing player from behind, below his waist.
  - Clipping is not usually called within 3 yards of the line of scrimmage and between the offensive tackles.

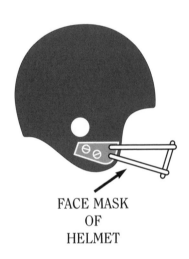

FACE MASK
OF
HELMET

- The penalty for clipping is a loss of 15 yards.

- If a player blocks an opposing player from behind, but not below the waist, the foul is ILLEGAL USE OF THE HANDS.

    1. The penalty for illegal use of the hands is a loss of only 10 yards.

    2. Clipping has a more severe penalty because of the greater chance of injury by the "low" block.

- DELAY OF GAME — The center of the offensive team fails to snap the ball within 40 seconds after the end of the previous play.

    - If the clock stopped due to an interruption of the flow of the game (such as team or TV time outs, an injury, change of possession or measurement) the referee will signal (and blow his whistle) to resume action. The center must snap the ball within 25 seconds of the referee's signal.

    - A PLAY CLOCK at each end of the field shows how many seconds remain before a delay of game is called.

    - The penalty for delay of game is a loss of 5 yards.

- GRASPING FACE MASK — A player pulls the face mask of an opposing player's helmet.

    - Can cause severe neck injuries.

    - The normal penalty yardage is a loss of 5 yards.

    - If the foul is intentional (called FLAGRANT), such as twisting or pulling the face mask, it is a 15-yard penalty and an automatic first down for the offensive team.

- ENCROACHMENT — A player makes contact with an opposing player after the center touches the ball but before he snaps it.

    - The penalty for encroachment is a loss of 5 yards.

ILLEGAL CONTACT

- OFFSIDE — A player is beyond his line of scrimmage when the ball is snapped.
  - The penalty for offside is a loss of 5 yards.
  - Defensive linemen sometimes jump offside when they are fooled during the quarterback's signal-calling (CADENCE), as to when the center will hike the ball.
- OFFENSIVE HOLDING — An offensive player, other than the ballcarrier, grabs (holds) an opponent. This includes encircling a defender with one's hands or arms.
  - This penalty is generally committed by an offensive lineman while attempting to block a defensive lineman.
  - The penalty for offensive holding is a loss of 10 yards.
  - An offensive holding foul that occurs in the offensive team's end zone is a safety.
- DEFENSIVE HOLDING — A defensive player grabs (holds) an offensive player other than the ballcarrier or a blocker.
  - This penalty usually is committed (before a pass is thrown) by a defensive back or linebacker holding a back or receiver who is trying to get in a position to catch the ball.
  - The penalty for defensive holding is a loss of 5 yards and an automatic first down.
- ILLEGAL CONTACT — During a passing play, a defender commits one of the following fouls resulting in a loss of 5 yards and an automatic first down:
  - Makes contact with an eligible receiver more than once, *within* 5 yards past the line of scrimmage or
  - Makes contact with an eligible receiver once, *more than* 5 yards past the line of scrimmage.
- ILLEGAL MOTION — The offense commits one of the following fouls resulting in a loss of 5 yards:
  - A man in motion is moving *toward* the line of scrimmage when the ball is snapped.
  - Two or more players are in motion when the ball is snapped.

INELIGIBLE RECEIVER DOWNFIELD

- FALSE START — The offense commits one of the following fouls resulting in a loss of 5 yards:
  - An interior lineman moves before the snap after he is in a SET POSITION (a stationary, motionless position such as a three-point stance with one hand and both feet touching the ground).
    1. If a defensive player enters the neutral zone before the snap, causing the offensive player(s) *directly in front of him* to move, a false start is not called. Instead, the defense is charged with NEUTRAL ZONE INFRACTION.
  - An offensive player simulates the start of a play before the ball is centered (such as a wide receiver moving prematurely).
- INELIGIBLE RECEIVER DOWNFIELD — An interior lineman goes past the line of scrimmage before a pass is thrown during a passing play.
  - No foul should be called if the interior lineman:
    1. Is beyond the line of scrimmage while surging forward blocking an opponent.
    2. Is beyond the line of scrimmage while surging forward blocking an opponent, loses contact with that opponent, but does *not* advance or move laterally.
  - The penalty for an ineligible receiver downfield is a loss of 5 yards.
- BALL ILLEGALLY TOUCHED — A forward pass is first touched or caught by an interior lineman or by an eligible receiver who stepped out of bounds during the play.
  - If a forward pass is first touched or caught by an interior lineman behind the line of scrimmage it is treated as an incomplete pass (a loss of down and the next play begins at the line of scrimmage).
  - If a forward pass is first touched or caught by an interior lineman beyond the line of scrimmage the penalty is a loss of 10 yards or the

BALL ILLEGALLY TOUCHED

play can be treated as an incomplete pass (a loss of down and the next play begins at the line of scrimmage), whichever the defense chooses.

– If an eligible receiver steps out of bounds, comes back onto the playing field, and is the first player to touch or catch a forward pass, the play is treated as an incomplete pass (unless the defense intercepts the ball). This is true even if the receiver was forced out of bounds by a defender.

– If an eligible receiver or a defender first touches a forward pass, all offensive players are eligible to catch the pass.

• INTENTIONAL GROUNDING — To avoid being sacked for a loss, the passer throws a forward pass that could never be caught. Remember, after an incomplete pass the offense begins its next play at the line of scrimmage.

– Intentional grounding will not be called if the quarterback is *out of the pocket* and throws a pass that lands near or beyond the line of scrimmage, even if he is about to be sacked.

– Intentional grounding is a loss of down and a penalty of whichever is greater:

  1. loss of 10 yards, or

  2. loss of the number of yards behind the line of scrimmage where the passer threw the ball.

– If intentional grounding takes place in the offensive team's end zone, it is a safety.

– To stop the clock near the end of a half, quarterbacks are allowed to receive the snap and *immediately* throw the ball into the ground for an incomplete pass. Intentional grounding will not be called.

• PASS INTERFERENCE — A player significantly hinders his opponent's opportunity to gain or retain position to catch or intercept a forward pass.

– If contact between opposing players is a result of both players attempting to catch

PASS INTERFERENCE

the ball, pass interference most likely will not be called.

- Once a pass is touched, pass interference is not called. Suppose a pass was tipped into the air by the split end, a defender could push the receiver to try to catch the ball.

- The penalty for offensive pass interference is a loss of 10 yards.

- When defensive pass interference is called, the next play begins at the spot of the foul (as if the pass was completed) and it is an automatic first down.

  1. If defensive pass interference occurs in the defending team's end zone, the next play begins at the 1-yard line (or half the distance to the goal if the line of scrimmage was within the defending team's 2-yard line).

  2. Defensive pass interference is not called behind the line of scrimmage.

- Pass interference should not be called when the pass is obviously uncatchable by the receiver and his defender(s).

- FACE GUARDING — A player with his back to the ball waves his arms in front of the receiver or defender—a form of pass interference that does not involve contact.

● UNNECESSARY ROUGHNESS — An uncalled-for act such as tackling a player who is obviously out of bounds or jumping on a player who is on the ground.

  - The penalty for unnecessary roughness is a loss of 15 yards. If an official believes the foul was too violent, he could EJECT the player from the game, forcing him to stay in his team's dressing room for the rest of the game.

  - If the foul is called on the defensive team, the penalty is also an automatic first down.

● RUNNING INTO OR ROUGHING THE KICKER — A player makes avoidable contact with the opposing team's punter or kicker.

UNSPORTSMANLIKE CONDUCT

• •

*Former Chicago Bear
Duke Hanny had a problem.
His wedding day was on the day of a
Bears home football game, so he asked
Coach George Halas if he could skip
the game. Halas responded with
an emphatic, NO!*

*What a dilemma! The wedding was
being held in Rockford, Illinois nearly a
three-hour drive from Chicago.*

*During the opening kickoff, Hanny
ran up to an opponent and socked him in
the mouth. The Bears were given an
unsportsmanlike conduct foul and
because it was flagrant, Hanny was
ejected from the game.*

*Hanny ran to the locker room,
got dressed and drove quickly to
Rockford to say "I do."*

– The penalty protects those players who are in a vulnerable position during a kick or punt.

1. The penalty for running into the kicker, which involves mild contact, is a loss of 5 yards.

2. The penalty for roughing the kicker, when "rough" contact is made with the opposing team's punter or kicker, results in a loss of 15 yards and an automatic first down.

– Unless an official considers the contact unnecessary roughness, running into or roughing the kicker is not called when:

1. The opponent who makes contact touched (called BLOCKED) the kick.

2. The snap touches the ground before it is kicked.

3. The opponent who makes contact was blocked into the kicker.

4. The punter attempts a QUICK KICK— punting the ball when it is not obvious that a punt is to be made.

● ROUGHING THE PASSER — A defender hits the quarterback after he throws the ball and the contact could have been avoided or minimized.

– If a quarterback is hit by a defensive lineman running toward him just after he releases the ball, roughing the passer should not be called. Most officials would rule that the defender's momentum unavoidably carried him into the quarterback.

– The penalty for roughing the passer is a loss of 15 yards and an automatic first down.

● UNSPORTSMANLIKE CONDUCT — A foul that the official considers lacking good sportsmanship.

– Unsportsmanlike conduct includes:

1. Using abusive language or gestures to officials, opponents or teammates.

2. A defensive player uses a teammate or opponent to boost himself up while attempting to block a kick.

Mention the name Conrad Dobler to a defensive player in the 1970's, and that player will immediately flinch. Dobler, who played with the St. Louis Cardinals, New Orleans Saints and Buffalo Bills as an offensive guard, had a reputation for the following: biting fingers, punching stomachs, kicking shins, grabbing face masks and spitting at players.

After a game against the Cardinals, ROOKIE (first-year) defensive tackle Jim Pietrzak of the New York Giants went up to Dobler for a friendly chat: "I went up to Dobler and wished him good luck in the playoffs. He turned around and punched me in the throat."

3. A punter, placekicker or holder fakes being hit by a defensive player in an attempt to have a foul called on the defender.

4. Punching or kicking an opponent.

– The penalty for unsportsmanlike conduct is a loss of 15 yards.

– If a player celebrates excessively or in a pre-meditated manner, then a loss of 5 yards for unsportsmanlike conduct will be assessed.

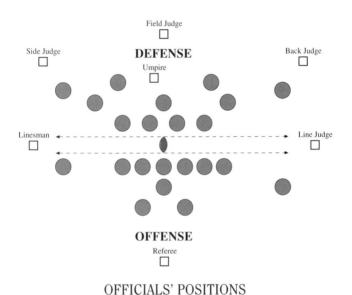

OFFICIALS' POSITIONS

OFFICIALS

Seven men who ensure that each team obeys the rules of the game.

- REFEREE — The main official who makes the final decision in disagreements that occur.

  - Blows his whistle to start play before a kick-off or after a time out.

  - After a foul is called, he explains the options of accepting or declining the penalty to the "fouled" team's captain. Using a cordless microphone and visual signals, the referee notifies the spectators of the captain's decision.

  - Before the snap, the referee stands behind the offensive backfield.

- UMPIRE — Has primary authority over the equip-ment and players' actions on the line of scrimmage.

  - Before the game, he inspects the equipment of the players to make sure it is not dangerous.

    1. Casts, guards or braces worn by play-ers must have ⅜-inch foam rubber or similar protective material.

    2. Coaches must notify the umpire before the game if any of their players will be wearing anything potentially danger-ous.

  - Counts the number of the offensive players on the field before each play.

  - Stands about 5 yards beyond the line of scrimmage between the hash marks.

- LINESMAN — Responsible for penalties that take place prior to or during the snap such as offside, encroachment and illegal motion. In addition, he helps out in determining other fouls that occur near the line of scrimmage soon after the snap, including ineligible receiver downfield and holding.

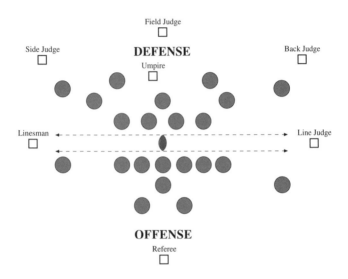

OFFICIALS' POSITIONS

•••

In 1965, Kansas City Chief tight end, Fred Arbanas, had his glass eye pop out during a collision with an opponent. The referee, Tommy Bell, picked it up and gave it to Arbanas, and commented on his bravery.

Bell then asked Arbanas what he would do if his other eye was injured. Arbanas responded, "Mr. Bell, I'd become a referee just like you."

- Works with the chain gang to make sure the measuring sticks are aligned properly on the sideline.

- Stands near one sideline at the line of scrimmage and usually switches sides after halftime.

- LINE JUDGE — Responsible for the timing of the game, especially if the game clock becomes inoperative.

  - Notifies home team's locker room when five minutes remain in the halftime intermission.

  - Stands across from the linesman and helps with the linesman's infraction responsibilities.

- BACK JUDGE — Responsible for action that takes place in the defensive backfield.

  - Counts the number of defensive players on the field before each play.

  - Stands 20 yards in back of the line judge.

  - During field goal attempts, stands under one of the uprights to determine if the kick is successful.

- SIDE JUDGE — Has same responsibilities as the back judge except he is on the opposite side of the field.

- FIELD JUDGE — Responsible for covering the action on a punt return and long passes.

  - Uses the 40/25 second play clock to determine if the delay of game penalty should be called.

  - Notifies the visiting team's locker rooms when five minutes remain in the halftime intermission.

  - Stands about 25 yards beyond the line of scrimmage even with the right offensive guard.

  - During field goal attempts, stands under one of the uprights to determine if the kick is successful.

COMMON OFFENSIVE STRATEGIES

Five ways an offense may react to a defense's success in sacking the quarterback:

- SCREEN PASS — A pass over the onrushing defenders to a back or end who has a "protective screen" of blockers in front of him.

  - Here's how a screen pass works.

    1. The offensive linemen allow defensive linemen to run past them, toward the quarterback.

    2. The offensive linemen then run in front of a running back (or sometimes an end).

    3. The quarterback backs up and tosses the ball over the onrushing defenders to the running back who has a friendly "escort" in front of him.

  - Next time the defense might not rush the quarterback as hard with the possibility of a screen pass lodged in the back of their minds.

  - Good "acting" is necessary by the offensive linemen, making the defenders think they were able to legitimately get through the offensive line on their way to the quarterback.

  - Smart defenders will "read the screen pass" and follow the offensive linemen instead of always going to the quarterback.

- DRAW PLAY — In a passing situation (such as third down and over three yards to go) the quarterback drops back as if to pass, but hands the ball to a running back.

  - A draw play's success is based on the defenders focusing on the quarterback during what appears to be a pass play.

  - The offensive linemen block the defensive linemen toward the outside, which is usually the route they take anyway to get to the quarterback. This leaves the middle open for the draw play.

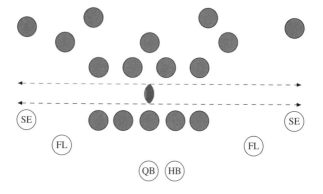

DEFENSE

SE

SE

FL

FL

QB HB

OFFENSE

RUN 'N' SHOOT

• •

Former Chicago Bears quarterback,
Mike Tomczak, kidded his teammate and
fellow-quarterback five-foot-nine Doug
Flutie with the following comment:
"We put in a special formation for him—
the sawed-off shotgun."

- Similar to the screen pass, the draw play slows down the defender's rush on a quarterback attempting to pass in plays that follow.

- SHOTGUN FORMATION — Quarterback lines up a few yards behind the center.

  - Gives the quarterback more time to pass before the defenders can get to him.

  - A screen pass from the shotgun formation is frequently effective.

  - Some teams use the shotgun formation in their RUN 'N' SHOOT offense.

    1. In the run 'n' shoot, four wide receivers are used, 2 flankers in the slot on each side of the field, and 2 split ends.

    2. The run 'n' shoot normally operates with only one running back and without a tight end.

    3. After the snap, the quarterback looks to see which of the four receivers (and running back) managed to escape a defender long enough to receive his pass.

- PLAY ACTION PASS — As the quarterback drops back to pass, he fakes a handoff to a running back. This "freezes" the onrushing defenders for a second, giving the quarterback more time to throw.

- ROLLOUT — Instead of dropping back into the pocket during a passing play, the quarterback runs to either the right or left side, away from the onrushing defenders.

SWEEP — Running back receives a handoff or lateral from the quarterback and runs around either end with offensive blockers leading the way.

- BOOTLEG — After faking a handoff or lateral, the quarterback sweeps around an end, usually hiding the ball on his outside hip.

OPTION PASS — At first looks like a sweep, but the running back has the option to pass the ball before he crosses the line of scrimmage.

New York Giants fans never forget November 19, 1978. On that day, the Giants were beating the Philadelphia Eagles 17-12. The Giants had third down and two yards to go from its own 29-yard line. Only 28 seconds remained in the game and the Eagles had no more time outs. There was no way the Giants could lose. Wrong!

Instead of instructing Giants quarterback Joe Pisarcik to kneel, assistant coach Bob Gibson wanted fullback Larry Csonka to run with the ball. Pisarcik took the snap and fumbled the ball as he was preparing for the handoff to Csonka. Eagles defensive back Herman Edwards picked up the fumbled ball and "danced" 20 yards into the end zone giving the Eagles a miraculous 19-17 victory.

Bob Gibson no longer had a job with the New York Giants.

- For an option pass to be successful, a defensive back is fooled into coming up to the line of scrimmage, ready to tackle the ballcarrier on an apparent sweep. The defensive back's assigned receiver is then open to catch the option pass.
- Many running backs who played quarterback in college or high school are more proficient with the option pass play because of their experience passing the football.

REVERSE — A running back or quarterback begins to sweep and then hands off or laterals to a wide receiver who is running in the opposite direction.

- Since the defense's pursuit is in the direction of the sweep, a reverse frequently leads to a large gain.
- Each defensive end usually has a responsibility to protect his side from a reverse.
- For more trickery, sometimes the wide receiver on a reverse will stop and throw an option pass.

QUARTERBACK SNEAK — When only a yard or less is needed for a first down or touchdown, the quarterback takes the ball from the center and follows behind the center or one of the guards.

QUARTERBACK "KNEEL" — Quarterback takes the snap and immediately drops to one knee *ending the play*. The quarterback watches the play clock and usually takes the snap just before a delay-of-game foul would be called.

- Intended to run out the clock during a half.
- Purpose is to reduce the possibility of a turnover.
- A "kneel" in the first half usually means:
    - The offense is on its own side of the field, too far away for a scoring opportunity.
    - The offense does not want to risk a play that could result in a turnover.
- If a "kneel" occurs near the end of the second half, it usually means that:
    - The offensive team is winning.
    - The offensive team does not want to risk a play that could result in a turnover.

Quarterback John Elway of the Denver Broncos is a master of the "two-minute" offense. He has engineered an amazing 31 game-saving, fourth quarter drives that have resulted in 30 wins and a tie. Seventeen times he's brought the Broncos from behind in the final three minutes, including eight times with less than a minute remaining.

– The defensive team does not have enough time outs to prevent the clock from running out while the offense has possession of the ball.

BOMB or FLY PATTERN — A receiver runs as far and as fast as he can, while the quarterback throws to him far downfield.

- The bomb is a quick way to gain a lot of yards in a short amount of time.
- At the end of a half, three or more receivers may run a fly pattern to the same area near the goal line. The quarterback throws the ball hoping one of his receivers will be able to outjump the defenders. This play is called a HAIL MARY.

TWO-MINUTE OFFENSE — Plays designed to take up very little time during the last two minutes of either half in an attempt to score.

- When the clock is running during the last two minutes, many teams go into a NO-HUDDLE OFFENSE (begin a play without first going into a huddle, listening for the quarterback's verbal signals at the line of scrimmage) or they will go into a huddle and call the next two plays.
- Some teams will go into a HURRY-UP OFFENSE (no-huddle) any time during the game to confuse the defense and limit the defense's substitution capability.

  – Many plays in a two-minute offense are designed to be passes near the sidelines. Here's why:
  – If the receiver catches the pass, he can step out of bounds which stops the clock.
  – The plays involve passes because if the receiver (or a defender) does not catch the ball, it is an incomplete pass which also stops the clock until the next play begins.
- The number of remaining timeouts in a half help the offense determine if a play other than a sideline pass should be called.
- During a two-minute offense, the offensive team is playing against the defense as well as the clock.

Former college and pro coach,
Frank Kush, described with disgust his
team's execution of its defensive strategy:
"We were in a nickel coverage, and we
played it like two cents."

COMMON DEFENSIVE STRATEGIES

NICKEL DEFENSE — When the defense expects a passing play, its coach may remove a defensive lineman or linebacker from the game and substitute a fifth defensive back to help cover receivers.

- If still another defensive back is inserted in the game, it is called a DIME DEFENSE.
- The nickel and dime defenses make it very difficult for a receiver to catch a pass because in most cases he will have two men defending against him, called DOUBLE COVERAGE.

MAN-TO-MAN DEFENSE — Each linebacker and defensive back is responsible for defending against a certain receiver. Excellent receivers may require double coverage.

ZONE DEFENSE — Each linebacker and defensive back is responsible for a certain area of the field, or zone, to cover.

BLITZ — Linebackers and/or defensive backs join the defensive linemen rushing in to sack the quarterback.

STUNT — A defensive lineman runs around another defensive lineman on the way to the quarterback to confuse the offensive linemen.

KEEP 'EM IN BOUNDS — During the last two minutes of a half, the defense tries to tackle the ballcarrier before he goes out of bounds to keep the clock running.

PREVENT DEFENSE — Defensive backs play far from the line of scrimmage making it difficult for a quarterback to complete a bomb for a long gain or a quick score.

- Allows the offense to complete short passes for small gains.
- Used primarily when the defense has a lead in the fourth quarter.
- Also used during the last play of the first half to defend against a hail-mary pass.

*During a playoff game
between the Dallas Cowboys
and the Cleveland Browns on December
28, 1969, the Cowboys had scored in the
fourth quarter, but were still losing 38-7.
The Cowboys decided that placekicker
Mike Clark should try an
onside kick.*

*As he approached the ball, his
teammates started running forward in
an effort to recover the onside kick.
Unfortunately, an important part of the
onside kick strategy did not happen.
Clark missed the ball!*

*Don't worry, Mike. Not many people
saw it—just the 70,000 fans in attendance
and the national TV audience.*

COMMON SPECIAL TEAMS STRATEGIES

ONSIDE KICK — During a kickoff, the kicking team attempts to kick the football just over ten yards in an attempt to recover the "free ball." Remember, once a kickoff touches a player on the receiving team or it travels 10 yards, it can be recovered by the kicking team.

- An onside kick is used near the end of a game when the kicking team is behind and can't afford to give the opponent's offense an opportunity to run out the clock.
- Rarely used early in the game, because if the receiving team recovers, its offense has excellent field position (approximately 40-45 yards from the goal line).

SQUIB KICK — During a kickoff, the ball is kicked on the ground to one of the SHORT MEN (the players on the receiving team who position themselves 20 or more yards in front of the end zone) instead of long and in the air to a kick returner.

- A squib kick is done to prevent an opposing team's great kick returner from running back the kickoff a long way.
- Many times a placekicker will kick the ball without a tee which causes the ball to bounce crazily, making it difficult for a short man to pick it up.

COFFIN CORNER PUNT — A punter punts the ball from near MIDFIELD (the 50-yard line) and tries to angle it so that the ball will go out of bounds as close to the 1-yard line as possible.

- A successful coffin corner punt puts the receiving team in poor field position.
- If the ball crosses the goal line before it goes out of bounds, it is a touchback and the receiving team's offense begins first and ten at its own 20-yard line.

- If the ball goes out of bounds before it crosses the goal line, then the receiving team's offense begins first and ten at the yard line where the ball went out of bounds.

- To give the punter a better angle at the coffin corner (the area on the field where the sideline meets the goal line), the punting team will sometimes intentionally cause a delay-of-game foul.

  - The penalty gives the punter an extra 5 yards in his coffin corner punt attempt.

  - Sometimes, the opposing team refuses the penalty so that the punter will not have the advantage of a better angle.

POOCH — A punter from near midfield punts the ball high into the air hoping it will touch the ground within the 10-yard line where a teammate can down the ball before it enters the end zone.

- A successful pooched punt puts the receiving team in poor field position.

FAIR CATCH KICK — After a punt returner or kickoff returner signals for a fair catch and catches the ball, his team has the option to kick a field goal from that yard line.

- The defenders must be at least 10 yards from the ball during the kick.

- If no time is remaining in the period when the fair catch is made, the field goal attempt is still allowed to take place.

	Dallas	NY Giants
First downs	21	16
Rushes-yards	36-182	35-130
Passing	157	183
Punt Returns	3-79	1-29
Kickoff Returns	1-12	2-36
Interceptions Ret.	0-0	2-54
Comp-Att-Int	24-30-2	16-25-0
Sacked-Yards Lost	4-23	3-24
Punts	5-36	6-36
Fumbles-Lost	2-1	4-3
Penalties-Yards	4-22	8-49
Time of Possession	38:35	32:09

INDIVIDUAL STATISTICS

Rushing: Dallas, Smithson 32-168, Aiken 2-8, Colton 2-6. New York, Hamlin 30-114, Meganson 2-11, Simpson 2-4, Bunson 1-1.

Passing: Dallas, Aiken 24-30-2-180. New York, Simpson 16-25-0-207.

Receiving: Dallas, Smithson 10-81, Johnson 6-47, Novellus 4-19, Irvine 3-50, Colton 1-3. New York, Callison 6-58, Hamlin 3-47, Crone 3-31, Pierson 2-41, Meganson 1-21, McCartney 1-9.

Missed Field Goals: Dallas, Murphy 43. New York, Trandowski 45, 53.

Dallas	3	9	0	8	3	-	**23**
New York	0	7	10	3	0	-	**20**

First Quarter
Dal - FG Murphy 32, 10:23.

Second Quarter
Dal - Smithson 5 pass from Aiken (kick failed), 7:34.
NY - Crone 8 pass from Simpson (Trandowski kick), 9:16.
Dal - FG Murphy 36, 15:00.

Third Quarter
NY - Bunson 1 run (Trandowski kick), 9:01.
NY - FG Trandowski 29, 13:40.

Fourth Quarter
NY - FG Trandowski 32, 4:50.
Dal - Perez 67 punt return (Cole pass from Aiken), 8:48.

Overtime
Dal - FG Murphy 41, 10:44.
Attendance: 77,653.

GAME SUMMARY

A complete summary of the scoring and statistics of a football game. It appears in the sports page of the newspaper in addition to the narrative highlights of the game.

The following statistics are shown for each team in the game summary.

- First downs — Total number of times a team's offense achieved a first down.

- Rushes-yards — Number of plays the offense ran with the ball (called RUSHING) and the total number of yards gained on those plays.

- Passing — Total number of yards the offense gained completing forward passes minus the total number of yards the offense lost because of sacks (see below).

- Punt Returns — Number of punts returned and total number of yards gained returning those punts. The yardage is measured from the yard line where the punt is caught to the yard line where the play ends.

- Kickoff Returns — Number of kickoffs returned and total number of yards gained returning those kickoffs. The yardage is measured from the yard line where the kick is caught to the yard line where the play ends.

- Interceptions Ret. — Number of interceptions by the defense and total number of yards gained returning those interceptions. The yardage is measured from the yard line where the pass is caught to the yard line where the play ends.

- Comp-Att-Int — Number of forward passes the offense completed and attempted and the number that was intercepted.

- Sacked-Yards Lost — Number of times the quarterback was sacked and total yards lost by those sacks.

- Punts — Number of punts and the average number of yards per punt.

	Dallas	NY Giants
First downs	21	16
Rushes-yards	36-182	35-130
Passing	157	183
Punt Returns	3-79	1-29
Kickoff Returns	1-12	2-36
Interceptions Ret.	0-0	2-54
Comp-Att-Int	24-30-2	16-25-0
Sacked-Yards Lost	4-23	3-24
Punts	5-36	6-36
Fumbles-Lost	2-1	4-3
Penalties-Yards	4-22	8-49
Time of Possession	38:35	32:09

INDIVIDUAL STATISTICS

Rushing: Dallas, Smithson 32-168, Aiken 2-8, Colton 2-6. New York, Hamlin 30-114, Meganson 2-11, Simpson 2-4, Bunson 1-1.

Passing: Dallas, Aiken 24-30-2-180. New York, Simpson 16-25-0-207.

Receiving: Dallas, Smithson 10-81, Johnson 6-47,Novellus 4-19, Irvine 3-50, Colton 1-3. New York, Callison 6-58, Hamlin 3-47, Crone 3-31, Pierson 2-41, Meganson 1-21, McCartney 1-9.

Missed Field Goals: Dallas, Murphy 43. New York, Trandowski 45, 53.

Dallas	3	9	0	8	3	-	23
New York	0	7	10	3	0	-	20

First Quarter
Dal - FG Murphy 32, 10:23.

Second Quarter
Dal - Smithson 5 pass from Aiken (kick failed), 7:34.
NY - Crone 8 pass from Simpson (Trandowski kick), 9:16.
Dal - FG Murphy 36, 15:00.

Third Quarter
NY - Bunson 1 run (Trandowski kick), 9:01.
NY - FG Trandowski 29, 13:40.

Fourth Quarter
NY - FG Trandowski 32, 4:50.
Dal - Perez 67 punt return (Cole pass from Aiken), 8:48.

Overtime
Dal - FG Murphy 41, 10:44.
Attendance: 77,653.

- Fumbles-Lost — Number of times a team fumbled and the number of those fumbles that were lost to the opposing team. A team's muffs are also included in this category.
- Penalties-Yards — Number of times a team was penalized and total number of yards lost by those penalties.
- Time of Possession — Total time (in minutes and seconds) a team had possession of the football.

The following statistics are shown for the top individual performers on each team:

- Rushing — The number of times an offensive player (usually a running back) ran the ball and the total yards gained.
  - When a player's rushing total is over 100 yards, that is considered an excellent performance.
- Passing — The number of times a player (usually a quarterback) completed a forward pass to a teammate, how many were attempted and how many were intercepted. Also, the total number of yards gained passing is listed.
  - When a player's completed passes total more than 300 yards, that is considered an excellent performance.
- Receiving — The number of times a receiver caught a forward pass and the total number of yards gained receiving those passes.
  - When a player gains more than 100 yards receiving, that is considered an excellent performance.

Missed Field Goals — The game summary includes the name of the kicker on each team who had an unsuccessful field goal attempt, and the number of yards from where he kicked the ball to the goal posts on each attempt.

The game summary includes the number of points scored by each team in the four quarters (and the over-

	Dallas	NY Giants
First downs	21	16
Rushes-yards	36-182	35-130
Passing	157	183
Punt Returns	3-79	1-29
Kickoff Returns	1-12	2-36
Interceptions Ret.	0-0	2-54
Comp-Att-Int	24-30-2	16-25-0
Sacked-Yards Lost	4-23	3-24
Punts	5-36	6-36
Fumbles-Lost	2-1	4-3
Penalties-Yards	4-22	8-49
Time of Possession	38:35	32:09

INDIVIDUAL STATISTICS

Rushing: Dallas, Smithson 32-168, Aiken 2-8, Colton 2-6. New York, Hamlin 30-114, Meganson 2-11, Simpson 2-4, Bunson 1-1.

Passing: Dallas, Aiken 24-30-2-180. New York, Simpson 16-25-0-207.

Receiving: Dallas, Smithson 10-81, Johnson 6-47, Novellus 4-19, Irvine 3-50, Colton 1-3. New York, Callison 6-58, Hamlin 3-47, Crone 3-31, Pierson 2-41, Meganson 1-21, McCartney 1-9.

Missed Field Goals: Dallas, Murphy 43. New York, Trandowski 45, 53.

Dallas	3	9	0	8	3	-	23
New York	0	7	10	3	0	-	20

First Quarter
Dal - FG Murphy 32, 10:23.

Second Quarter
Dal - Smithson 5 pass from Aiken (kick failed), 7:34.
NY - Crone 8 pass from Simpson (Trandowski kick), 9:16.
Dal - FG Murphy 36, 15:00.

Third Quarter
NY - Bunson 1 run (Trandowski kick), 9:01.
NY - FG Trandowski 29, 13:40.

Fourth Quarter
NY - FG Trandowski 32, 4:50.
Dal - Perez 67 punt return (Cole pass from Aiken), 8:48.

Overtime
Dal - FG Murphy 41, 10:44.
Attendance: 77,653.

time period).

For each quarter, the scoring details are listed.

- When an offensive player scores a touchdown on a passing play, the game summary lists the team, the receiver, the passer and the number of yards from the line of scrimmage to the goal line.

- When an offensive player scores a touchdown on a running play, the game summary lists the team, the scorer's name and the number of yards from the line of scrimmage to the goal line.

- When a player returns a punt, kickoff, fumble or interception for a touchdown, the game summary lists the team, the scorer's name and the number of yards from where he gained possession of the ball to the goal line.

- When a player kicks a field goal, the game summary lists the team, the kicker's name and the number of yards from where he kicked the ball to the goal posts.

- After a touchdown when there is a successful PAT kick, the game summary lists the team, the name of the placekicker followed by the word "kick." If the kick is unsuccessful, the word "failed" or "blocked" appears next to the placekicker's name.

- After a touchdown when there is a successful two-point PAT conversion, the game summary lists the team, the player who scored and the passer if it was a passing play. If the attempt is unsuccessful, the word "failed" appears next to either "run" or "pass."

- The game summary lists the time elapsed in the quarter when each score took place.

TOUCHDOWN PASS — Some game summaries list the number of touchdown passes thrown and received.

- An offensive player (usually the quarterback) is credited with throwing a touchdown pass if he completes a forward pass to a teammate who runs into the end zone or catches it in the end zone.

- An offensive player is credited with catching a touchdown pass if he catches a forward pass from a teammate while in the end zone or subsequently runs into the end zone.

LEAGUE STRUCTURE AND
TEAM STANDINGS

The NATIONAL FOOTBALL LEAGUE (NFL) is the professional league of football.

The STANDINGS show the position of each team within its division based on its wins, losses and ties.

The NFL has two conferences, with three divisions in each conference.

NATIONAL FOOTBALL CONFERENCE	*AMERICAN FOOTBALL CONFERENCE*
NFC	*AFC*
EAST DIVISION	**EAST DIVISION**
ARIZONA CARDINALS	BUFFALO BILLS
DALLAS COWBOYS	INDIANAPOLIS COLTS
NEW YORK GIANTS	MIAMI DOLPHINS
PHILADELPHIA EAGLES	NEW ENGLAND PATRIOTS
WASHINGTON REDSKINS	NEW YORK JETS
CENTRAL DIVISION	**CENTRAL DIVISION**
CHICAGO BEARS	CINCINNATI BENGALS
DETROIT LIONS	CLEVELAND BROWNS
GREEN BAY PACKERS	HOUSTON OILERS
MINNESOTA VIKINGS	PITTSBURGH STEELERS
TAMPA BAY BUCCANEERS	
WEST DIVISION	**WEST DIVISION**
ATLANTA FALCONS	DENVER BRONCOS
NEW ORLEANS SAINTS	KANSAS CITY CHIEFS
LOS ANGELES RAMS	LOS ANGELES RAIDERS
SAN FRANCISCO 49ERS	SAN DIEGO CHARGERS
	SEATTLE SEAHAWKS

In 1995 the NFL will expand, adding the Carolina Panthers and the Jacksonville Jaguars (called EXPANSION TEAMS). The league may decide to restructure its divisions to geographically accommodate the new and existing teams. For example, it may decide to move Arizona and Dallas from the East to the West Division of the NFC, move Atlanta from the West to the East

Division of the NFC, and add Jacksonville to the East Division of the NFC.

Common abbreviations used in the standings:

- W (Wins) — The total wins by the team during the season.
- L (Losses) — The total losses by the team during the season.
- T (Ties) — The total ties by the team during the season.
- Pct. (Winning Percentage) — The ratio of a team's total wins (plus half of its ties) to total games played.
- PF (Points For) — The total number of points scored by a team during the season.
- PA (Points Against) — The total number of points given up by a team during the season.
- NFC or AFC — The total wins, losses and ties a team has in games played against teams in its own conference.
- Div (Versus Division) — The total wins, losses and ties a team has in games played against teams in its own division.

National Conference									
EAST	W	L	T	Pct.	PF	PA	Home	NFC	Div
NY Giants	12	4	0	.750	376	229	6-2-0	10-2-0	7-1-0
Philadelphia	11	5	0	.688	288	205	6-2-0	9-3-0	5-3-0
Washington	7	9	0	.438	259	295	3-5-0	5-7-0	3-5-0
Dallas	7	9	0	.438	326	269	4-4-0	6-8-0	4-4-0
Arizona	4	12	0	.250	230	345	3-5-0	3-9-0	1-7-0
CENTRAL	W	L	T	Pct.	PF	PA	Home	NFC	Div
Chicago	10	6	0	.625	298	292	5-3-0	8-6-0	4-4-0
Detroit	9	7	0	.563	277	290	4-4-0	7-5-0	6-2-0
Minnesota	9	7	0	.563	340	282	6-2-0	6-6-0	4-4-0
Tampa Bay	7	9	0	.438	234	230	3-5-0	5-7-0	3-5-0
Green Bay	5	11	0	.313	237	376	3-5-0	4-8-0	3-5-0
WEST	W	L	T	Pct.	PF	PA	Home	NFC	Div
LA Rams	11	5	0	.688	453	261	6-1-0	8-3-0	4-2-0
San Francisco	8	8	0	.500	317	343	4-4-0	6-6-0	3-3-0
Atlanta	6	10	0	.375	316	385	4-4-0	5-7-0	4-2-0
New Orleans	5	11	0	.313	221	367	3-5-0	3-9-0	1-5-0

PROFESSIONAL FOOTBALL SEASON CYCLE

TRAINING CAMP — The 6 to 8 week period from the middle of July to the beginning of September when players get into shape, preparing for the regular season. Teams frequently practice twice during the day in the hot summer sun and have meetings at night.

- Not only do teams practice among themselves, but they also play 4 or 5 PRE-SEASON GAMES against other teams.
- During training camp, coaches decide who will be on the team (sometimes called the ROSTER) for the beginning of the regular season.

Regular Season — the 16-game schedule each team plays beginning in September.

- Each team plays the other teams within its division twice during the season—once at each team's home field. The rest of the regular season opponents vary each year.
- The primary objective of each team is to finish in first place, having the best winning percentage of all teams in its division, and advancing to the playoffs.
- The secondary objective of each team is to have one of the top three winning percentages among the teams in its conference who did not finish in first place in their division. These teams are called WILD CARDS, and also advance to the playoffs.
    - In the sample standings that are illustrated, Philadelphia, Detroit and Minnesota would be the wild card teams for the NFC. They have the top three percentages among the non-division winners in the NFC.

National Conference

EAST	W	L	T	Pct.	PF	PA	Home	NFC	Div
NY Giants	12	4	0	.750	376	229	6-2-0	10-2-0	7-1-0
Philadelphia	11	5	0	.688	288	205	6-2-0	9-3-0	5-3-0
Washington	7	9	0	.438	259	295	3-5-0	5-7-0	3-5-0
Dallas	7	9	0	.438	326	269	4-4-0	6-8-0	4-4-0
Arizona	4	12	0	.250	230	345	3-5-0	3-9-0	1-7-0
CENTRAL	W	L	T	Pct.	PF	PA	Home	NFC	Div
Chicago	10	6	0	.625	298	292	5-3-0	8-6-0	4-4-0
Detroit	9	7	0	.563	277	290	4-4-0	7-5-0	6-2-0
Minnesota	9	7	0	.563	340	282	6-2-0	6-6-0	4-4-0
Tampa Bay	7	9	0	.438	234	230	3-5-0	5-7-0	3-5-0
Green Bay	5	11	0	.313	237	376	3-5-0	4-8-0	3-5-0
WEST	W	L	T	Pct.	PF	PA	Home	NFC	Div
LA Rams	11	5	0	.688	453	261	6-1-0	8-3-0	4-2-0
San Francisco	8	8	0	.500	317	343	4-4-0	6-6-0	3-3-0
Atlanta	6	10	0	.375	316	385	4-4-0	5-7-0	4-2-0
New Orleans	5	11	0	.313	221	367	3-5-0	3-9-0	1-5-0

Playoffs — Three weekends of play after the regular season to determine who will represent each conference in the Super Bowl. The team with the better winning percentage is the home team (except a division winner is always the home team when playing a wild card).

- Weekend one — The 3 wild card teams and the division winner with the lowest percentage in each conference (Chicago in the sample standings that are illustrated) play. The other 2 division winners have the week off.

- Weekend two — Two more games are played within each conference. Each game includes a winner of the previous week's playoff games against one of the remaining division winners.

- Weekend three — The winners of the two games played within each conference during the previous week play for the conference championship.

SUPER BOWL — After the conference championships, this game matches the two winners.

- The Super Bowl determines the world champion of professional football.

- Super Bowls have traditionally earned some of the highest television ratings in history.

COLLEGE FOOTBALL RULE DIFFERENCES

College football has *no overtime period*. If the score is tied after the 60 minutes of regulation play, the game ends as a tie. The NFL has *sudden death overtime.*

PAT conversions start at the *3-yard line* in a college game instead of the *2-yard line,* the starting point in an NFL game.

If a college defensive player gains possession of the ball during a PAT, and he or a teammate crosses the offense's goal line (97 yards away from the original snap) during the same play, his team is awarded two points. Professional football rules do not permit the defense to score on a PAT.

Many penalties differ in terms of yardage. For example, defensive holding is a *10-yard penalty* in college football, but only a *5-yard penalty* in professional football.

The illegal contact penalty in professional football does not apply to college football. A college defensive player *can* have contact (but not holding) with an offensive eligible receiver more than five yards past the line of scrimmage (except if the pass is already in the air).

A play ends in college football when any part of the ballcarrier's body, other than his hands or his feet, touch the ground. Unlike the NFL, it does not matter if the ballcarrier fell on his own without contact by a defender; the play still ends.

For a reception to count in college football, only *one foot* (not *two* as in the NFL) needs to be inbounds while catching the ball. If the player jumps in the air to catch the ball, only *one* foot (not *two* as in the NFL) needs to be inbounds when first touching the ground.

When a college team achieves a first down, the *clock*

stops until the chain gang has set up for the next series of downs. In a professional game, the *clock continues to run* when a team achieves a first down.

Once a college referee signals to start the play, the offense has *25* seconds to snap the ball or it will be charged with the delay of game penalty. In professional football, if the clock did not stop due to an interruption of the flow of the game (such as team or TV time outs, an injury, change of possession or measurement), the offense has *40* seconds after the previous play ended to snap the ball.

Each of the hash marks for a college football game are *60 feet* from the nearest sideline. For a professional game, the hash marks are *70 feet, 9 inches* from the nearest sideline. Some fields that are used for both college and football games may have both sets of hash marks on the field. Don't be confused. Remember that the hash marks closest to the center of the field are for professional football.

If a team wins the coin toss in a college football game, it can elect to have first choice in the second half which usually means it will receive the second half kickoff. The loser of the coin toss will then have first choice in the first half and it most likely will choose to receive the first half kickoff. Professional football does not give the winner of the coin toss the option to choose first in the second half.

- A college team cannot have more than 4 captains at the coin toss.
- A professional team is limited to 6 captains at the coin toss.

College football kickoffs start from the kicking team's *35-yard line*. NFL kickoffs start from the kicking team's *30-yard line*.

On an unsuccessful field goal attempt by a college kicker, the defensive team takes over on offense at the *line* of *scrimmage* of the kicking play, or the 20-yard line, whichever is furthest from the end zone. In the NFL, the defensive team takes over on offense on the yard line *where the ball was kicked,* or the 20-yard line, whichever is furthest from the end zone.

- If the opposing team touches the ball beyond the line of scrimmage, or if the field goal attempt is blocked and the ball ends up behind the line of scrimmage, the next play begins where the kicking play ends in both college and NFL football.

After a college player makes a fair catch, his team is *not* entitled to a fair catch kick. The fair catch kick *is* allowed in professional football.

When a college kickoff goes out of bounds without touching a member of the receiving team, the receiving team has three options:

- Its offensive series can begin at the yard line where the ball went out of bounds.
- Its offensive series can begin 30 yards from where the ball was kicked.
  - If the opposing team kicked off from its 35-yard line and the ball went out of bounds, the receiving team can start play on its own 35-yard line (30 yards from the spot of the kick).
- It can force the kicking team to re-kick from 5 yards back from the previous kick.
  - A receiving team during an NFL game does not have the option to force the opponents to re-kick.
  - In an NFL game, when an onside kick attempt goes out of bounds (or does not travel 10 yards):
    1. If it is the first attempt, the kicking team must re-kick from 5 yards back.
    2. If it is the second consecutive attempt, the receiving team takes possession at the yard-line where the ball went out of bounds (or where the ball ended up if it did not travel 10 yards).

In a college game, a period is always extended on a penalty that is accepted, *no matter which team committed the foul.* The NFL rules dictate that a period can be extended only if a penalty is against the *defense.*

- At the end of the first or third period, a professional offensive team that was fouled can choose to have the penalty enforced at the beginning of the next period. (Maybe the wind direction is more favorable to the offensive team).

In college football, there is no two-minute warning as there is in professional football.

During a college kickoff, there must be at least 4 players on each side of the kicker. There is no corresponding requirement in an NFL game.

- This difference is important to note when the kicking team is attempting an onside kick.

In a college game, if a backward pass (lateral) touches the ground and is then recovered by a defensive player, the play *automatically ends* at the spot of recovery. In the NFL, a defensive player *can advance* a recovered lateral even if it had touched the ground.

In a college game, if an eligible receiver is forced out of bounds by a defender, he can immediately come back inbounds and try to catch a pass. In the NFL, once a player goes out of bounds (even if he was forced out) he is no longer eligible to catch a pass unless the ball is first touched by an opponent or an eligible teammate.

If a college player goes out of bounds (without being forced out) he becomes eligible to catch the ball only if the pass first touches an opponent. In the pros, a player who goes out of bounds is no longer eligible to catch a pass unless the ball is first touched by an opponent or an eligible teammate.

During a punting play, *all members* of a college punting team may leave the line of scrimmage once the ball is snapped. The pros allow only the *2 players* lined up closest to each sideline to run downfield once the ball is snapped.

A quarterback is an eligible receiver in college football. He is only eligible in the NFL if he does not receive a hand-to-hand snap directly from the center.

A play does not end in college football when the quarterback is in the grasp and control of a defender behind the line of scrimmage. In the NFL, the play does end. NFL quarterbacks are more protected under professional football regulations.

In the NFL, a coach may communicate with his quarterback using an in-helmet electronic system. College football does not permit such a system.

Halftime intermission in college football is *20* minutes, while only *12* minutes in the NFL.

● ●

Here's something that most fans do not know. After a college team scores a touchdown (and attempts the PAT conversion) or a field goal, the opposing team has the option to receive or kick during the kickoff that follows. Nearly all the time, the team will choose to receive the kick-off so that its offense will get the ball (and the opponent's offense will not) to try to score.

The NFL requires that after a team scores a touchdown or a field goal, the opposing team must receive during the kickoff that follows.

COLLEGE FOOTBALL TEAM GOALS

Currently there is no playoff system in major college football after each team completes its regular season schedule.

- Initial goal — Most colleges are in a CONFERENCE made up of a number of teams whose goal is to finish in first place in its conference.
    - The Southeastern Conference has two divisions, with a playoff game between the division winners to determine the conference champion. In the future, other conferences may also set up two divisions.
    - Some colleges are INDEPENDENTS and are not affiliated with a conference. The University of Notre Dame is an example of an independent.
- Intermediate goal — Go to a BOWL GAME in December or January.
    - The bowl games are held in cities throughout the country. The most notable ones take place on New Year's Day.
    - The winner of most conferences is automatically invited to a bowl game.
    - Other teams with six or more wins during the regular season may also be invited to a bowl game.
- Final goal — Win the national championship.
    - After all the bowl games have been played, sportswriters and football coaches vote in separate polls on who should be crowned champion.
        1. Associated Press — Poll of broadcasters and sportswriters.
        2. USA Today/Cable News Network — Poll of football coaches.
    - The vote is based on each team's won-loss record and the strength of the other teams on its schedule.
    - Sometimes, the two polls have different winners resulting in two national champions.

INDEX

FOOTBALL QUIZ #1

1. *In an NFL game, if the teams are tied after four quarters, what happens?*
    a. The game ends in a tie.
    b. The first team to score in the 15-minute over-time period wins. If no team scores, then it is a tie.
    c. The teams continue playing and the game ends only when a touchdown is scored.
    d. Each team runs 4 plays from midfield, and the team that ends up closest to the opposing team's goal line, wins.

2. A team begins a play at its own 37-yard line and the quarterback runs the ball to his 43 where a line-backer throws him backwards to the ground on his 41-yard line. *At what point does the next offensive play begin?*
    a. At the 37-yard line.
    b. At the 41-yard line.
    c. At the 43-yard line.
    d. At midfield.

3. *After a team scores a safety, what happens?*
    a. The team that scored can either punt or kick off from its 20-yard line.
    b. The team that did not score can either punt or kick off from its 20-yard line.
    c. A coin flip determines which team is to receive the ball.
    d. A time out is charged to the team that scored.

4. A team returns a kickoff to the opposing team's 48-yard line, and on the next play the quarterback completes a 13-yard pass to his tight end. *What is the situation for the next play?*

> a. Second down, 23 yards to go, from the opposing team's 35-yard line.
> b. First down, 10 yards to go, from the opposing team's 35-yard line.
> c. First down, 10 yards to go, from its own 39-yard line.
> d. Second down, 7 yards to go, from its own 39-yard line.

5. *Of the following, who is usually the biggest player?*

> a. Defensive Back.
> b. Wide Receiver.
> c. Quarterback.
> d. Defensive Lineman.

6. *When a quarterback changes a play at the line of scrimmage because of the defensive alignment this is called a(n)...*

> a. Down.
> b. Audible.
> c. Blitz.
> d. Sneak.

7. On third down, 6 yards to go in an NFL game, the flanker catches a 33-yard pass from the quarterback by diving for it on the opposing team's 23-yard line. There is not a defender within 8 to 10 yards of him; so he gets up and runs to the end zone untouched. *What happens on the next play?*

> a. First down, 10 yards to go, from the opposing team's 23-yard line.
> b. The PAT conversion attempt.
> c. The offensive team most likely punts.
> d. First and goal from the 1-yard line.

8. *When the third quarter of a game ends, what takes place at the beginning of the fourth quarter?*

    a. A coin flip to determine which team receives the ball on the kickoff.
    b. The game ends if a team is leading in the score by more than 35 points.
    c. Whichever team kicked off at the beginning of the third quarter receives the ball on the kickoff.
    d. The teams switch sides and play resumes at the yard line where the last play ended.

9. *Of the following, who usually catches the most passes for the offense?*

    a. Quarterback.
    b. Tackle.
    c. Split end.
    d. Guard.

10. Of the following, who usually gains the most rushing yardage?

    a. Halfback.
    b. Center.
    c. Flanker.
    d. Tight end.

ANSWERS TO FOOTBALL QUIZ #1

1. (b) A tie at the end of regulation play in the NFL results in sudden death overtime; the first team to score, wins. However, in a pre-season or regular season game, if neither team scores within the 15-minute overtime period, the game ends in a tie.

2. (c) The quarterback's forward progress stopped at the 43-yard line; so that is where the play ended.

3. (b) A safety is the only scoring play that:
   - Entitles the team that scored to receive the ball.
   - Gives the team that gave up the safety the option to either punt or kick off.
   - Requires the kickoff or punt to take place at the kicking team's own 20-yard line.

4. (b) After the kickoff the offense starts with a first down and 10 yards to go. Because the offense gained 13 yards when it only needed 10, it earned another first down at the opposing team's 35-yard line.

5. (d) A defensive linemen requires more bulk than non-linemen because they have to be physically equipped to constantly deal with the large offensive linemen at the line of scrimmage.

6. (b) An audible describes a quarterback changing the play at the line of scrimmage after reading the defense.

7. (b) A play does not end if an NFL ballcarrier falls and is not touched by an opponent on his way down or while he is down. Therefore, the ballcarrier can get up and score a touchdown. That means the PAT is next.

8. (d) Teams always switch sides between the third and fourth quarter (and the first and second quarter). The first play of the fourth quarter begins on the yard line where the last play of the third quarter ended.

9. (c) A split end normally catches more passes than interior linemen (who are usually ineligible receivers) and the quarterback (who throws instead of catches passes).

10.(a) A halfback generally carries the ball more on running plays than the flanker and tight end (who both specialize in catching passes) and the center (who as an interior lineman, spends nearly all of his time blocking for running backs such as the half-back).

FOOTBALL QUIZ #2

Pretend you are an NFL team's coach in the following situations:

1. Your opponent's defense is consistently pressuring your quarterback attempting to pass. *What play might you call on 3rd down, 6 yards to go?*

   a. Draw play.
   b. Screen play.
   c. Play-action pass.
   d. Any of the above.

2. Your team has the ball, third down, one-half yard to go for a first down on the opposing team's 35-yard line. Your team's center is one of the best blockers in the league. *What play might you call?*

   a. Quarterback sneak.
   b. Screen pass.
   c. Flanker reverse.
   d. Draw play.

3. Your team is losing 21-19. It is fourth down and goal to go for your team on the opposing team's 8-yard line. There are 23 seconds left in the game. *What should your team do?*

   a. Punt.
   b. Pass the ball to an end or a back in the end zone.
   c. Sweep.
   d. Attempt a field goal.

4. The situation is the same as in number 3 above, except your team is losing 21-17. *What should your team do?*

    a. Punt.
    b. Pass the ball to an end or a back in the end zone.
    c. Sweep.
    d. Attempt a field goal.

5. Your team is winning 21-20. It is third down, 7 yards to go from your own 17-yard line. Thirty seconds remain in the game as the referee signals the ball ready to play. The opposing team had called their last time out after the previous play. *What should you do?*

    a. Pass the ball for a first down.
    b. Attempt a field goal.
    c. The quarterback should immediately kneel upon receiving the ball from the center.
    d. Throw a bomb.

6. It is third down, 12 yards to go for the opposing team. *What might you do defensively?*

    a. Substitute an extra defensive back for a linebacker.
    b. Blitz your free safety.
    c. Blitz one of your linebackers.
    d. Any of the above.

7. It is first down, 10 yards to go for the opposing team on its 27-yard line. Your team is winning 28-24 with 12 seconds left in the game. *What would you do defensively?*

    a. Prepare to block a field goal attempt.
    b. Play a prevent defense.
    c. Have 8 men on the line of scrimmage to pressure the quarterback.
    d. Prepare for a running play.

8. On a third down and 6 yards to go from its own 37-yard line, the opposing team threw an incomplete pass. The referee indicates there was an illegal motion penalty called on your opponents. There are 8 minutes left in the first quarter of a scoreless game. *What would you do?*

    a. Accept the penalty.
    b. Decline the penalty.
    c. Call time out.
    d. Ask for an offsetting penalty.

9. Your team is winning 34-28. There are 18 seconds left in the game and the opposing team has called its final time out. Your team has fourth down and 11 yards to go from your own 6-yard line. *What would you do?*

    a. Tell your punter to step out of the end zone with the ball for a safety.
    b. Run a halfback sweep to try to run out the final 18 seconds.
    c. Punt the ball to put them in poorer field position.
    d. Throw a bomb.

10. Your team is losing by 2 points after just scoring a touchdown and PAT with one minute left in the game. Your team has one time out remaining. *What would you do?*

    a. Kick the ball deep to them, hoping they'll fumble.
    b. Squib kick it so their deep kickoff returners cannot run the ball back for a touchdown.
    c. Kick the ball out of bounds.
    d. Attempt an onside kick.

ANSWERS TO FOOTBALL QUIZ #2

1. (d) A draw play, screen pass and play-action pass are used to offset a strong rush by the defense. So any of these plays would be appropriate.

2. (a) A quarterback sneak is generally successful when a team needs less than a yard for a first down, especially if the center or a guard is an outstanding blocker. This type of running play takes less time because there is no handoff, so the defense has less time to react.

3. (d) Because your team is only losing by 2 points, you should try to win the game with a 3-point field goal attempt.

4. (b) Your team is losing by 4 points, so a 3-point field goal will not help. Therefore, you should try to score a touchdown to win the game.

5. (c) With only thirty seconds remaining and forty seconds allowed between plays, the idea is to run a safe play that does not stop the clock. In this situation most teams' quarterbacks will kneel once they receive the snap and the referee will blow his whistle signifying the end of the play.

6. (d) When the offense is in an obvious passing situation, a blitz can be used to sack or pressure a quarterback. Also, putting in an extra defensive back can make it more difficult for the quarterback to find an open receiver.

7. (b) A field goal won't help the opposing team because they are losing by 4 points. So, it must travel 73 (100-27) yards in 12 seconds for a touchdown to try to win the game. For that to happen, it most likely will try to complete a bomb. Your team should be in a prevent defense to minimize the chance of the probable long pass being completed.

8. (b) By declining the penalty you will force the opponents to punt the ball. If you accept the penalty, the

opposing team will still have a chance to make a first down on the third down, 11 yards to go play.

9. (a) Congratulations if you got this right as many coaches don't think about this strategy. Late in the game, it really doesn't make much difference if your team is winning by 6 points or 4 points. In either case, the opponents cannot tie with a field goal and they can win with a touchdown and a one-point PAT.

So instead of punting from your own end zone (where the opponents might block the kick), give up the safety, narrowing the deficit insignificantly from 6 to 4, and punt or kickoff from your 20-yard line (without fear of the kick being blocked).

10. (d) An onside kick has to be attempted in this situation when you don't have enough timeouts to prevent the opposing team from running out the clock (remember that 40 seconds may elapse between plays unless the clock is stopped), before you can regain possession.

BIBLIOGRAPHY

Adams, John. *1994 NCAA Football Rules and Interpretations.* Overland Park: National Collegiate Athletic Association, 1994.

Aiken, Miles. *American Football: The Records.* Great Britain: Guinness Books, 1985.

Benagh, Jim. *FOOTBALL: Startling Stories Behind the Records.* New York: Sterling Publishing, 1987.

Braine, Tim. *The Not-So-Great Moments in Sports.* New York: William Morrow, 1986.

Chieger, Bob. *Football's Greatest Quotes.* New York: Simon & Schuster, 1990.

Foehr, Donna Poole. *TOUCHDOWN: A Guide to Understanding and Enjoying Football.* Bloomfield Hills: Franklin Press, 1993.

Nash, Bruce. *The Football Hall of Shame.* New York: Pocket Books, 1986.

Nash, Bruce. *The Football Hall of Shame 2.* New York: Pocket Books, 1990.

Seeman, Jerry. *1994 Official Playing Rules of the National Football League.* New York: National Football League, 1994.

Treat, Roger. *The Encyclopedia of Football.* Garden City: Dolphin Books, 1979.

COMMON OFFICIAL SIGNALS

TOUCHDOWN, FIELD GOAL, OR SUCCESSFUL TRY · SAFETY · FIRST DOWN · BALL ILLEGALLY TOUCHED · TIME OUT

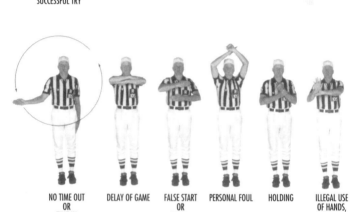

NO TIME OUT OR TIME IN WITH WHISTLE · DELAY OF GAME · FALSE START OR ILLEGAL FORMATION · PERSONAL FOUL · HOLDING · ILLEGAL USE OF HANDS, ARMS, OR BODY

PENALTY REFUSED, INCOMPLETE PASS, PLAY OVER, OR MISSED GOAL · PASS JUGGLED INBOUNDS AND CAUGHT OUT OF BOUNDS · ILLEGAL FORWARD PASS · INTENTIONAL GROUNDING OF PASS · INTERFERENCE WITH FORWARD PASS OR FAIR CATCH

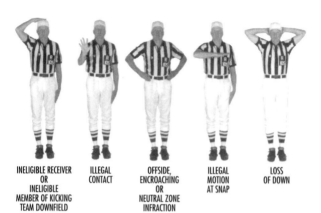

INELIGIBLE RECEIVER
OR
INELIGIBLE
MEMBER OF KICKING
TEAM DOWNFIELD

ILLEGAL
CONTACT

OFFSIDE,
ENCROACHING
OR
NEUTRAL ZONE
INFRACTION

ILLEGAL
MOTION
AT SNAP

LOSS
OF DOWN

TOUCHING A
FORWARD PASS
OR
SCRIMMAGE KICK

UNSPORTSMANLIKE
CONDUCT

PLAYER
DISQUALIFIED

UNCATCHABLE
FORWARD
PASS